We are at the point of an economic revolution, and con... increasingly moved by the injustice of trade and the human and environmental costs of big corporate profits. Francesca Romana Rinaldi and Salvo Testa's book *The Responsible Fashion Company* goes a long way to pulling together existing research on sustainable fashion and is full of positive examples of better practice in luxury fashion. An inspiring read for new economists, intellectuals, fashion people and consumers, alike.

Safia Minney, MBE, Founder and CEO, People Tree

The Responsible Fashion Company offers a comprehensive picture of the challenges and opportunities of sustainability in the global fashion industry. The discussion about the role of the neo-consumer and the 'LOHAS' practitioners is particularly inspiring. Across industries, enterprises have seen their sustainability initiatives fail or only develop into symbolic action because of a lack of consumer buy-in. *The Responsible Fashion Company* gives useful examples of how sustainable business models may be created in the necessary dialogue with consumers. Read, learn from others and develop your own innovative way of doing business the right way.

Mads Øvlisen, Chairman of the UN Global Compact's Advisory Group on Supply Chain Sustainability

Today, themes such as ethics and moral values are getting to the heart of society. Not only as an individual approach but also from a corporation's perspective. This coincides with the will of driving change in the social environment. Companies in particular play a key role in this, and it is essentials for managers, professionals, researchers and students to have access to in-depth data... I love this book because it provides a clear framework of how the fashion industry is moving, business and managerial models, and rich case studies.

Rossella Ravagli, Head of Corporate Sustainability & Responsibility, Gucci

As part of an industry which leaves a massive footprint on people and planet, the growing challenge we face is balancing the fast-moving demands of the fashion world with the realities of a production system which struggles to keep pace. This book is a refreshing and relevant overview of the facts, bringing to life the dilemmas and challenges underlined by examples of how businesses can drive positive change whilst using it to their competitive advantage.

Rachel Hearson, Account Manager, Fairtrade Foundation UK

Full of inspiring ideas and concrete case studies, this book is for anyone who wants to know how ethics and fashion can work together to define a new social agreement. It is actually possible to go beyond the capital/labour dichotomy and reconcile environmental conservation and personal dignity, without renouncing either to profit or beauty.

Sara Tommasiello, Finance, HR & CSR Manager, Monnalisa Group

Rinaldi and Testa's book addresses a fundamental but neglected issue inherent in the fashion sustainability debate: the fragile and apparently impossible balance between beauty, values, and the economic imperative; the model it proposes merits applause. The book is a must read for managers and academia determined to contribute to a better world through responsible fashion business practices and education.

Michela Ornati, Program Director, Fashion & Luxury Sustainability Summer School, University of Applied Sciences and Arts of Southern Switzerland (SUPSI)

This book fills a gap in the market for students and employees of fashion who want to understand the industry's current cultural context and the role sustainability now plays within this. It also provides a good overview of sustainability models and initiatives that are relevant to fashion, as well as a breadth of brand case studies which help underline that strong ethics and environmental considerations now underpin the success of leading commercial companies.

Allanna McAspurn, CEO, MADE-BY

As the fashion industry continues to hit the headlines due to its negative impact on both the environment and the people working to make our clothes, this book provides a focused and in depth overview of the challenges affecting the sector. From cradle-to-cradle processing and triple bottom line strategy to maintaining brand integrity, the authors effectively illustrate the way businesses can address these challenges and move towards a responsible and commercial value chain.

Victoria Waugh, Director, Ethical Fashion Forum and SOURCE Consultancy

All the ideas and cases shown in this book highlight how the aesthetic is linked to ethics. In a world where natural resources are coming closer to an end each day, it doesn't make any sense to think about fashion as a linear economic activity, disregarding its social, cultural and environmental aspects. More than ever it is necessary to see that the fashion industry – if well oriented – can work as a contemporary tool towards the development of an awareness through which sustainability is central. And this book represents a breaking point against false dichotomies that often lead to shallow analysis about what fashion is – and its potential. Thanks to this book, we can see how it is possible to reconcile one of the most important industries in the world – one that generates more 30 million jobs – with best practices.

Oskar Metsavaht, Founder and Creative Director of Osklen and Instituto-E

Far-sighted and ahead of its time: the authors clearly define the new paradigms that we need and which, willingly or unwillingly, we shall have to apply in a not too distant future, perhaps sooner than we realise.

Carlo Petrini, Founder of Slow Food

This book provides everything you need to know about how to manage responsibility in the fashion industry.
Diana Verde Nieto, Co-Founder and CEO, Positive Luxury

Nudie Jeans started as a dream about not having to compromise, making the jeans we want at the same time as bringing a consideration for the environment and human rights into every aspect of products. This book describes many good examples of how this is happening in our industry.
Henrik Lindholm, CSR Manager, Nudie Jeans

The Responsible Fashion Company
Integrating Ethics and Aesthetics in the Value Chain

THE
RESPONSIBLE
FASHION
COMPANY

Integrating Ethics and Aesthetics in the Value Chain

FRANCESCA ROMANA RINALDI

SALVO TESTA

Greenleaf
PUBLISHING

Published by
Greenleaf Publishing Limited
Aizlewood's Mill, Nursery Street
Sheffield S3 8GG, UK
www.greenleaf-publishing.com

Printed in the United Kingdom
Printed and bound by CPI Group (UK) Ltd, Croydon, CR0 4YY

Translated from the original Italian edition by Loredana Maria Rinaldi.
Cover adapted from a design by Juri Ceccotti.

British Library Cataloguing in Publication Data:
    A catalogue record for this book is available from the British Library.
        ISBN-13: 9781783532216 [paperback]
        ISBN-13: 9781783532193 [hardback]
        ISBN-13: 9781783532223 [PDF ebook]
        ISBN-13: 9781783532209 [ePub ebook]

～

I dedicate this book to my dear friend Alfredo and his smile.
Francesca Romana Rinaldi

～

I dedicate this book to my father who has always
taught me, without too many words, that what
is Right comes before what is Useful.
Salvo Testa

～

Contents

Foreword

by Carlo Petrini
Founder of Slow Food

No doubt, I am not an expert in fashion, but in my area of expertise, gastronomy, I have seen so many trends go out of fashion. The word 'fashion' is of course intended in its most common sense, that of trends: the culinary and production styles which have become increasingly *de rigueur*, especially in haute cuisine, given the considerable media profile enjoyed by some great (or not so great) chefs.

This somewhat limited point of view is achieved if we understand 'gastronomy' in its classic sense, a world that mainly consists of chefs and gourmet enthusiasts in search of excellence and a natural physiological, legitimate, pleasure that has too often been an end in itself. Gastronomy in its classic sense is not necessarily just haute cuisine; I am surely referring to a world that includes restaurants, good pubs and home cooks, a sort of big club of enthusiasts of which the majority, unfortunately, have for too long looked only at the result: the deliciousness of what is in the dish.

For quite a few years now, in the Slow Food movement we have been trying to develop an old concept of gastronomy entirely based on recipes and the like. If we return to the definition given by Jean-Anthelme Brillat-Savarin in his *The Physiology of Taste* of 1825, we immediately realise that gastronomy is actually something more complex, interdisciplinary, which includes other fields of knowledge and of human life. Brillat-Savarin wrote:

> Gastronomy is the intelligent knowledge of whatever concerns man's nourishment [...] So it is the motive force behind ploughmen, growers of the vine, and the great family of cooks, under whatever title or qualification they may disguise their employment as preparers of food. Gastronomy pertains: to natural history, through the classification of foodstuffs; to physics, through the various processes of analysis and catalysis to which it subjects them; to cookery, through the art of preparing dishes and making them agreeable to the taste; to commerce, through its quest for the cheapest possible means of buying what it consumes and the most profitable market for what it has to sell; to political economy, through its resources and means of exchange established between nations.

Starting with this old definition, with Slow Food we have inaugurated a new way of thinking, tasting, producing, buying and dealing with food, as well as setting it once again at the centre of our lives. We have summarised it in a motto, which seems simple but it is not at all so: 'good, clean and fair'. It represents a new definition for food quality, which takes into account the organoleptic goodness searched for by classic gourmets (good) and extends it further, introducing elements of culture, ecology and sustainability (clean), and elements of social justice concerning both food producers and consumers (fair). In concrete terms, it includes all the disciplines listed by Brillat-Savarin with the addition of some new ones, which are more stringent and topical for these postmodern times.

Food is one of the elements which most affects the lives of men (positively or negatively, from pleasure to health, from environmental balance to labour exploitation) and also the Earth. It is a mistake to redesign its system in excessively industrialist or reductionist terms, the child of a market economy that has revealed limits and flaws which have been placed under the spotlight by the many structural crises that the world is going through. If a few years ago drawing attention to food sustainability seemed to many to be an excessive concern typical of environmental Cassandras, today the scenario has changed completely. We have to admit that the motto 'good, clean and fair' has gained some success and has begun to circulate more, anticipating what have become legitimate concerns, and looking to a future that may not be so rosy without radical changes. This way of reasoning is spreading within the world's food system—from agriculture to the table—so much so that it has become, in some cases, a 'trend'. We have noted strong interest from other more diverse sectors, proving that values related to food are indeed universal. If food is what most binds us with a direct line to Nature and its balances, other productive sectors are not exempt from this connection and also face a structural crisis caused by not having complied with certain limits, basing their actions on the assumption that growth was infinite.

There is no mistake that it is time to conceive and implement new paradigms in our activities. It is the time to be reconciled with the Earth without denying or giving up pleasure, wellbeing and an aesthetics that has nothing to lose if it adheres to ethical principles. In my opinion, this is a challenge that is not so difficult to win.

For this reason I am particularly interested in the book you are now about to read, so far-sighted and ahead of its time: the authors clearly define the new paradigms that we need and which, willingly or unwillingly, we shall have to apply in a not too distant future, perhaps sooner than we realise. Because after all, I am convinced of what Edgar Morin says: 'If *everything must start all over again*, then *everything has* already started all over again.'

Introduction

καλὸς καὶ ἀγαθός
(Beauty and goodness).
Plato

The book you are about to read concerns a transition period: we can say goodbye to the great certainties of ideologies, linear development and the Enlightenment faith in progress, and welcome a new era of complexity, uncertainty and systematic doubt. We are now in the so-called era of 'liquid modernity'. The paradigms and business models of consumption are changing: this revolution is also evident in the fashion sector.

In the last decade the consumer has started to get used to buying clothes and accessories as if they were sweets: the 'democratic' concept of fashion has allowed increasingly lower prices to be paid thanks to increasingly reduced costs, to the extent that guaranteeing good quality and a fair production process is becoming unsustainable. This is another price to pay.

This book also speaks of a revolution: the new consumer—or perhaps it would be better to say the 'consum-actor' or 'consum-author'—is contributing to rethinking, rebuilding and redesigning the rules of the market. The buyer wants to be more informed about a product's origins, its production procedures and the labour employed in that process. This revolution has even led to the birth of a strong new opposition between 'to be' and 'to use', inaugurating an era of critical and participatory consumption.

The most important fast fashion chains, such as Zara and H&M, have questioned the traditional production logic and timing based on two seasonal collections (spring/summer and autumn/winter), by increasing the number of deliveries to shops and by dramatically reducing time-to-market[1] and lead-time.[2] The increasing delocalisation of production has generated an increasing globalisation of the supply chain. All of this has stimulated a corresponding surge towards new attitudes for companies, starting with increased attention to quality and a will to control the entire value chain. Recently, a new *slow fashion* movement has started to appear; a return to the past as evidenced by models of supply based on proximity of manufacturing and the valorisation of craftsmanship.

So how is the sector changing? What are the new managerial models necessary to manage a company in this varied context?

Our thesis is that, in order to continue being competitive, companies must adopt a new managerial and entrepreneurial model that involves a medium to long-term perspective and takes into account all the parties involved, namely the stakeholders—from the environment to society, culture, the media, institutions and legislation—placing values and ethics at the centre.

The idea of the book was born and grew with Bio-Fashion,[3] a blog created to give voice to companies, associations and opinion-formers on topics pertaining to environmentally friendly fashions and lifestyles. About a hundred interviews have been collected in around

---

1   The time it takes to go from initial product design to delivery to the shop.
2   The time it takes from the moment the company receives an order to delivery to the shop.
3   A blog created in 2010 by Francesca Romana Rinaldi (http://bio-fashion. blogspot.com).

three years of research and the sphere of activity expanded: environmental sustainability and activities with an environmental impact are, indeed, only one of the topics in the book (Chapter 3). Right from the blog's first post and from the first page of this book, the objective was to devise a new model capable of integrating the aesthetic, competitive and ethical variables of fashion by placing people at the centre (consumers, employees, suppliers, etc.) along with their interaction with various stakeholders along the value chain.

Despite great interest in the issue of responsibility in fashion from academics, students, professionals and managers at a national and international level, at this point in time there are very few books on CSR (Corporate Social Responsibility) with an industry-specific approach. This gap in the literature has motivated our desire to explore the topic by using our combined experience in the field as consultants, lecturers and tutors for numerous projects with multinational, small and medium-sized companies.

This book takes readers on an exploratory journey starting with the concept of CSR and sustainable development. Chapters 1 and 2 introduce the new value proposition and new models for creating value, referring to CSR from a multisector perspective. The subsequent chapters analyse the relationships of mutual exchange between the fashion company and its various and connected contexts.

The main idea is this: *long-term economic balance in the company can only be achieved by incorporating economic short-term objectives, which are essential for the remuneration of capital and labour, with other non-economic objectives referring to the relationship with the environment, society, culture, the media, institutions, legislation and, most of all, the perspective of values and ethics.*

This thesis is part of a topical debate on the company's important social role, in light of the failure of an economic development model that has only emphasised immediate economic and financial results. The model for a responsible company conceptualises an economic long-term balance based on compatibility with the environmental and social context. A company operating in the fashion sector must be ready to answer a series of questions. How can it reduce its environmental impact? How can it contribute to the economic development of the territory (district, region or nation) in which it is present? How can it interact with stakeholders through new media? How can it repay culture, its main source of inspiration in terms of aesthetic codes? Given the current globalisation and localisation process, how can it respect the rights of workers and develop their skills in all the countries in which production takes place? How can it respect consumers? In responsible fashion, the environmental and social macrocontexts interface with businesses in order to gain systemic balance: the fashion company draws inspiration and obtains resources from the two contexts and then returns compensations and contributions consistent with expectations and needs, in a logic of exchange. For instance, this can be achieved through programmes to reduce environmental impact, to promote the territory, for healthy and stimulating working environments, for the quality of the products guaranteed to the consumer, and for the promotion of culture through philanthropic deeds, artistic collaborations, funding, donations and corporate museums.

In each chapter we have chosen examples of best practice to describe the ratio of exchange between a company and a single context: these are companies that decided years ago to pursue the difficult challenge of incorporating ethics, aesthetics and economy into the value chain. We have also included contributions by opinion-formers (CEOs, associations, journalists, etc.) whom we interviewed in person. Through this case-oriented approach we show how social and environmental responsibility must be seen not only as an innovative and qualifying business model *per se*, but also as the only way to ensure medium and long-term economic sustainability.

The fashion sector is slowly experiencing what has already occurred recently and suddenly in the food and wine sector (think of Slow Food[4]

---

4   See Section 2.8.

or Eataly,[5] for example), where handmade and high-quality products are radically changing the model of consumption with a return to values, meanings and production methods from the pre-industrial era which guarantees the quality and exclusivity of the product and also its traceability, but without nostalgia for the past, instead incorporating new requirements (including the intangible and emotional) and technologies in the product, in communication and in distribution (such as innovative fibres and packaging, social communication, e-commerce, etc.).

Chapter 3 investigates the relationship between fashion and the environment, Chapter 4 explores that between fashion and society, Chapter 5 is dedicated to the media, Chapter 6 to the relationship between fashion, art, culture and territory, Chapter 7 to that between fashion, legislation and institutions, and Chapter 9 to ethics.

In Chapter 8 the case of Brunello Cucinelli is analysed as a means of presenting a holistic view of the model of a responsible fashion company.

5 Eataly is an international chain of multi-brand stores. The brand brings together a group of small companies working in various areas of the food and wine sector: from the hard wheat pasta of Gragnano to the egg pasta of the Langhe region, from the water of the Maritime Alps to the wines of Piedmont and Veneto, from the oil produced in the Liguria area to Piedmont beef and, furthermore, traditional Italian cheeses and cured meats. Eataly offers the best local artisan products at affordable prices, minimising the distribution chain and creating a direct link between the producer and end distributor, bypassing the various intermediate links of the chain.

Credits

This book is the product of the personal interest, as well as the academic and professional research, of the two authors. Chapters 1–3 were written by Francesca Romana Rinaldi (Section 2.7 was written with Salvo Testa); the three central chapters were written by Francesca Romana Rinaldi in collaboration, respectively, with Stefano Pogutz (Chapter 4), Sissi Semprini (Chapter 5) and Nicoletta Giusti (Chapter 6); Chapter 7 was written entirely by Paolo Foglia and Chapter 8 by Salvo Testa; Chapter 9 was written by both authors (Salvo Testa wrote Sections 9.1 and 9.2; Francesca Romana Rinaldi wrote Sections 9.3 and 9.4.

Acknowledgements

We would like to thank all the people without whom this book would not have taken shape. In alphabetical order:

Erica Corbellini, friend and colleague, director of the Master in Fashion, Experience & Design Management at SDA Bocconi School of Management, who believed in the project from the start; Paolo Foglia, head of Research & Development of the Institute for Ethical and Environmental Certification (ICEA), for his support for the research carried out on this topic over the past three years and for writing Chapter 7; Nicoletta Giusti, Director, MSc in Fashion Design and Luxury Management at Grenoble Graduate School of Business, for accepting our invitation to collaborate on Chapter 6; Stefano Pogutz, professor of Green Management and Corporate Sustainability in the Department of Management and Technology at Bocconi University, for accepting the invitation to collaborate on Chapter 4; Sissi Semprini, founder of Greenbean, for having shared many ideas and her passion for wanting to give an account of a new way of communicating, and for having contributed to Chapter 5.

A special acknowledgement goes to those who have contributed to generating ideas for the book, in particular to Stefania Saviolo, director of the Luxury & Fashion Knowledge Center at SDA Bocconi; Zoe Romano; the entire Change Up team; Veronica Crespi, style consultant and creator of Rewardrobe, London; Marta Pesamosca (www.martstudio.it); Alfredo Mattiotto; Sara Francesca Lisot (http://iamgreenaddict.wordpress.com); Gianluca Pulsoni, literary and film critic (www.sigismundus.it); Laura Fazzini; Barbara Ceschi (www.behindthelabel.it); and finally, students Johan Christian Chen, Gergana Yotova, Zoya Yudina, Beatrice Panisi and Stella Richetti.

A special acknowledgement goes to Carlo Petrini, founder of Slow Food, for writing the Foreword.

We also thank all the people who have believed in the project and dedicated their time and attention during meetings, projects and interviews. In particular:

Giulia Iemmolo, legal expert on CSR issues in the Chinese market, Studio Pirola Pennuto Zei & Associati; Ilaria Pasquinelli, director of Texsture Limited, London; Roberta Rizzoli, PR and Press Office, Dr Hauschka Cosmesi-Wala Italia; Fausto Panni, managing director of Wala Italia; Alessandro Pulga, director of ICEA; Piero Sardo, president of the Slow Food Trust for Biodiversity; Andrea Illy, president and managing director of illycaffè; Claudia Reder, materials researcher at Material ConneXion Italia; Giusy Bettoni, founder of the showroom Creativity Lifestyle and Sustainable Synergy (CLASS); Ornella Bignami, founder of Elementi Moda; Alessandro Butta, of the Cooperativa La Campana (Montefiore dell'Aso, Ascoli Piceno); Jonas Eder-Hansen, development director, Danish Fashion Institute, Nordic Initiative Clean and Ethical (NICE); Irma Biseo, corporate partnerships and external relations director, WWF Italia; Stefano Cochis, general manager of Saluzzo Yarns (Sinterama Group) and creator of Newlife™; Sara Tommasiello, Finance and Control Manager, Human Resources, CSR Manager, Monnalisa; Oskar Metsavaht, founder and creative director of Osklen; Mario Campori, retail manager, Patagonia Europe; Isabelle Susini, environmental and CSR manager, Patagonia

Europe; Ilaria Venturini Fendi, founder and creative director, Carmina Campus; Elisabetta Facco, communication manager and PR, Carmina Campus; Monica Della Valle, head of image and communication for Gruppo Tod's; Safia Minney, CEO of People Tree; Beniamino Muroni, former PR manager, People Tree; Orsola de Castro, creative manager of From Somewhere and Reclaim To Wear, co-founder and curator of Estethica LFW; Marina Spadafora, creative manager of Auteurs du Monde; Gabriella Ghidoni, referral person for Quality and Relation with the producers of Auteurs du Monde and creator of the project Royah Design in Afghanistan; Rachel Hearson, account manager, Fairtrade Foundation UK; Chiara Tabaccanti, product manager in charge of cotton at Fairtrade Italia; Carla Lunghi, researcher in Sociology of Cultural Processes, Catholic University of the Sacred Heart, Milan; Luciana Delle Donne, CEO of Officina Creativa scs (whose brands include Made in Carcere and ER-RE); Luisa Della Morte, Cooperativa Sociale Alice; Rossella Ravagli, head of CSR and sustainability, Gucci; Antonio Batticciotto, manager of strategic development and new business, Malìparmi; Elisabetta Bettucchi, communication manager for Malìparmi; Annalisa Paresi, president of Malìparmi; Lucy Shea, chief executive, Futerra; Diana Verde Nieto, Positive Luxury; Filippo de Caterina, director of institutional communication, L'Oréal Italia; Andrea Francardo, product manager, IOU Project; Allanna McAspurn, CEO of Made-By; Susannah Ellis, communications manager, Historic Futures; Vincenzo Lianello, president of Gruppo Cooperativo GOEL, owner of the Cangiari brand; Giovanna Furlanetto, president of Furla and Fondazione Furla; Stefania Ricci, director of the Salvatore Ferragamo Museum; Brunello Cucinelli, founder and CEO of Brunello Cucinelli; Gaetano Rinaldi, national councillor for Italia Nostra; and Fiammetta Capecchi, lawyer at the legal firm Capecchi-Valerio.

Juri Ceccotti (http://juriceccotti.tumblr.com/), artist, illustrator and visualiser, created the book cover.

1

The new paradigms

If we could change ourselves, the tendencies in the world would also change. As a man changes his own nature, so does the attitude of the world change towards him. [...] We need not wait to see what others do.

Mahatma Gandhi

1.1 The new paradigms of consumption and information

We are witnessing a real revolution. This revolution starts with demand and leads us to rethink, rebuild and redesign the rules of the market: the definition of 'consumer' loses its meaning as it assumes the final stage of the transaction as a mere process of purchasing and consuming. It is better to describe the neo-consumer as a 'consum-actor' (Fabris 2008) or 'consum-author' (Morace 2008), a user but, at the same time, an active part of the complex consumption dynamics, increasingly one-to-one, in which the sceptre passed a long time ago from the brand to the consumer. The new consumption paradigm, as asserted by Fabris (2008), is described by the fact that 'consumers can be involved in the role of producer-designer-client because they have gained knowledge and awareness from which the company can learn a great deal, translating them into the development of goods and services'.

In recent years, some fashion brands—of different business models and positioning—have interpreted this evolution perfectly by launching projects which attempt to establish a new relationship with the neo-consumer. The use of new technologies and e-commerce has facilitated this process, assuring neo-consumers of their participation in the customisation of products. Some examples represent this evolution perfectly:

- Converse, with the 'Design Your Own' project, allows clients to personalise every detail of their trainers, and to order the shoes via the company's website for them to be delivered to their home two to three weeks later.

- Nike, with the 'NIKEiD' project, allows the upper, insole and laces of running shoes to be customised, and it is even possible to put an 'iD' on the shoe's tongue.

- Burberry, with the customised line called 'Bespoke', represents an example of luxury customisation. Clients can buy the trenchcoat of their dreams, after choosing every detail (fabric, colour, sleeves, lining, collar, buttons, metal parts, belt and label) from the comfort of their own home.

In his cult book *Societing*, Fabris (2008) summarised the characteristics of the neo-consumer as follows:

- *Polygamy and infidelity to the brand.* The new way of relating with the brand implies a progressive reappraisal of the brand's actual ideology and growing power for the consumer.

- *Nomadism.* Intended both literally, for the increasing amount of travel from one city to another and from one country to another, and metaphorically, for the 'continuous slalom among products, consumption styles, brands that are becoming the *modus vivendi* of the postmodern consumer […] could indeed be traditionalist in their choice of car and an experimenter in food, minimalist for house decor and exhibitionist in clothing, open to what is new with regards to intellectual consumption and conservative towards new technologies'.

- *Competences, needs and selectivity.* With the increase in both competition and available alternatives, as well as the transparency of product information guaranteed by the Internet, the neo-consumer is increasingly competent, demanding and selective. Today, consumers are informed (and increasingly want to be so) regarding the origin of the product, the production method and the type of labour used. Says Fabris: 'Ethics, the widespread request by producers and sellers for socially responsible behaviour, attention to the consumption chain even including the countries of origin of the raw materials, the production methods, the workers' fair salaries, the environmental impact due to production, right up to waste disposal' represent the new critical factors for establishing a successful and trusting relationship with the neo-consumer.

- *Price sensitivity.* This characteristic is also influenced by the increase in competition and available alternatives, as well as by the transparency of product information which is guaranteed by the Internet.

In addition to what Fabris describes, the change of paradigm includes an undeniably innovative way of consumption that can be summarised by the expression 'collaborative consumption',[1] introduced by Botsman and Rogers (2010) to establish a new era of critical consumption and participation: the era of sharing and of shared consumption. It is no coincidence that we are hearing terms such as car-sharing, bike-sharing, co-working, etc., more frequently. They are all based on the

---

1   See this video from the 2010 TEDxSydney conference in which Rachel Botsman introduces the criteria for collaborative consumption: www.youtube.com/watch?v=zpv6aGTcCl8.

same idea: sharing a space, product or service turns the concept of private property upside down.

If we look at the fashion sector, we can add more terms to the list— like barter; 'swap parties'; re-use and recycle—to reveal a new idea of consumption: a logic that is no longer individualistic but pertaining to a community, a consideration which includes more evaluation elements than just the price/quality ratio and aesthetics. What do all these terms have in common? Sustainability. In fact, speaking about shared consumption in fashion means looking at the environmental and social impact of the products.

In fact, all the characteristics of the neo-consumer described above are fully compatible with those of the consumer who is informed and shops mainly online:

- *Polygamy, infidelity to the brand and price sensitivity.* Brand infidelity is growing with the increasing number of channels through which one can obtain information and compare characteristics.

- *Nomadism.* The neo-consumer is a nomad even when choosing and using digital devices (smart phones, notebooks and tablet computers) to go online in order to obtain information and buy. Multichannel is the new mantra.

- *Competence, need and selectivity.* Thanks to information transparency guaranteed by the Internet, the neo-consumer can always be up to date regarding the origin of the product, the production method and the type of labour used.

Time magazine was among the first to speak about the revolution in consumption and information in this new era of the Internet, and dedicated the cover of its December 2006 issue[2] to this topic. In the context of this paradigm shift, what is the role of the Internet and social media? The Internet and social media are, respectively, the

---

2   http://content.time.com/time/magazine/0,9263,1101061225,00.html.

channel and the tool which are helping the new consumption paradigms become more pervasive (see Chapter 5).

1.2 The neo-consumer in fashion

The image of the neo-consumer, increasingly attentive to the environmental and social impact of products, continues to spread at an international level and belongs to the niche often known as 'cultural creatives' or even LOHAS (Lifestyles of Health and Sustainability).

When we speak of LOHAS we refer to a type of consumer that pursues, through daily choices, a lifestyle based on ecological sustainability and on attention to their own health and that of the planet. Consequently, when shopping, this consumer always chooses carefully, is aware of the importance of quality and of the origin of products, and prefers organic food. For example, LOHAS consumers realise that buying a piece of furniture made of tropical wood without a certificate of origin contributes to mass deforestation of the rainforests. So, if possible, they choose furniture that does have certification or is made using wood produced locally. LOHAS consumers are aware that, when buying a house belonging to energy efficiency class A, they are contributing to the reduction of greenhouse gas emissions, and so they opt for this kind of solution. When buying a car, LOHAS consumers also make a decision on the basis of sustainability criteria such as the amount of carbon dioxide emissions, the recyclability of materials and energy efficiency, because they realise that they can each make a difference and that, if the environment is protected, they are the ones who will benefit. In the United States, a study carried out in 2007 by the Natural Marketing Institute identified 40 million inhabitants as LOHAS. Japan, Singapore and Taiwan are the Asian countries with the highest diffusion of LOHAS.[3] In Europe, the

---

3   www.esseresostenibili.it/ambiente/consumatori-lohas/.

country with the greatest diffusion is Germany, where about a third of the population is identified as practising this lifestyle.

The common characteristics of LOHAS can be summarised by an attention to the environment, awareness, and respect for health and society. At the same time, these consumers do not want to boycott fashion and technology: this aspect distinguishes them from the classic 'eco' people. These characteristics are, in brief, the following:

- LOHAS consumers live mainly in urban areas.

- They do not think only about their own benefits, but also how their lifestyle has an impact on other people and the environment.

- They tend to buy organic products which comply with ethical standards, fair trade and sustainability.

- They have a hybrid lifestyle: they are in favour of technological development but love enjoying nature; they want to live life with a perfect psychophysical balance but think about the relationship with others; and they are realistic but open to spirituality.

- They want to be involved in the creative process of products.

Even if each country has its own specific qualities, it is valid to assume that this segment is growing.

In the absence of specific research on LOHAS consumers within the Italian market, some alternative data can be used as a proxy for our country:

- The increase in the number of consumer fairs and exhibitions (or sections thereof) specifically dedicated to sustainability (especially in the fashion, furnishing and design, and food and wine sectors) and the relative number of visitors.

- The increase in the number of websites and blogs dedicated to sustainability.[4]

4   For example, there are 39,300,000 results when searching for 'sustainability' on Google (September 2014).

Table 1.1 **Principal sustainable fashion fairs in Europe.**

Fair	City, country	First held (sustainability section)
Biofach	Nuremberg, Germany	1990
InNaTex	Wallau, Germany	1997
Heimtex til	Frankfurt, Germany	2000
Ethical Fashion Show	Paris, France Berlin, Germany	2004
Estethica	London, UK	2006
Premium/Green Luxury Area Pitti	Berlin, Germany	2007
Pitti Immagine Filati ('Equo Eco Friendly' section)	Florence, Italy	2008
Fa' la cosa giusta! ('Critical Fashion' section)	Trento, Italy Milan, Italy Palermo, Italy	2003 2008 2012
Alta Roma ('Ethical Fashion' section)	Rome, Italy	2008
TheKey.To	Berlin, Germany	2009
White ('Selection by CLASS' section)	Milan, Italy	2010
Ecoluxe	London, UK	2010
So Critical So Fashion	Milan, Italy	2011
MINT	Amsterdam, Holland	2012

Source: Adapted from Rinaldi (2011).

Evidence for the growing interest of the neo-consumer in sustainable fashion consists of events such as the Ethical Fashion Show, or the sections dedicated to this sector within 'non-specialist' fairs such as Pitti Immagine Filati. The principal fairs across Europe are summarised in Table 1.1.

The Danish Fashion Institute, through the NICE (Nordic Initiative Clean and Ethical) project and the nonprofit organisation, BSR, have produced a framework to clarify consumer commitment to fashion's sustainable consumption. The report, *The NICE Consumer: Toward a Framework for Sustainable Fashion Consumption in the EU* (Danish Fashion Institute and BSR 2012), describes how neo-consumers can play a significant role in the process of converting the fashion industry to more sustainable business models. Nevertheless, neo-consumers are currently hindered in their task by various factors:

- *Little awareness.* Fashion product buyers are not very aware of the impacts of consumption on society and on the environment.

- *Lack of transparency.* Inadequate access to information about products and the associated supply chain.

- *Poor supply.* A scarcity of more sustainable options in the sector in terms of price, variety of models and fashion content.

The NICE project aims to raise awareness of sustainable and responsible business models in the fashion industry. There are primarily four actions that the NICE consumer should take in order to achieve a more sustainable behaviour pattern, spread through the product's life-cycle:

- *Purchase phase.* Request garments that are more sustainable for the environment and for people, and choose more mindfully what to buy and from whom.

- *Consumption phase.* Improve the garments' care.

- *Post-consumption phase.* Adopt behaviours such as responsible recycling.

Copenhagen Fashion Summit 2014

The development of a concept and framework for sustainable consumption in fashion represents the concluding phase of a number of activities carried out over the past few years by the Danish Fashion Institute through the NICE project.

→

- Establishment of a NICE Consumer Advisory Group to help lead the project.

- Research aimed at empowering and influencing the choices and behaviours of consumers.

- Drafting of a NICE Consumer Change Framework defining the possible roles and actions of consumers, companies, governments and other involved parties to support sustainable consumption in fashion.

- Activation of a consultation process to obtain 'crowd-sourced' input and feedback, i.e. from the bottom.

- Launch of the framework, and presentation of results to the presidency of the European Union in the first half of 2012.

- Promotion of the framework during the UN Conference on Sustainable Development (Rio+20) held in Rio de Janeiro on 20–22 June 2012.

In May 2012, over a hundred students from the best design and business universities gathered in Copenhagen to present the results of research carried out interviewing some potential 'NICE consumers'. The manifesto resulting from this workshop, presented at the Copenhagen Fashion Summit 2012, can be summarised in seven requests from the neo-consumer:

- *Consumer solutions.* 'We demand that brands create memories, not junk.'

- *Cost.* 'We demand to see the total cost tag, instead of just the price tag.'

- *Communication.* 'We demand a voice for the consumer, a forum where they can ask their questions about sustainability and break through the jungle of communication.'

- *Convenience.* 'We demand that you cut the crap. Make sustainable fashion an easy choice.'

→

- *Consultation.* 'We demand the empowerment of retail staff with knowledge and pride. Pride + involvement = sense of community.'
- *Civil society.* 'We demand a link between the society of makers and the society of wearers. Rebuild trust!'
- *Coolness.* 'We demand that designers are empowered to make sustainability a creative possibility—and turn hippie into Gaga!'

Some requests are difficult to implement on a large scale (for example, that of showing the detail of the cost of the product, not just the price), but others are easy to implement (for example, the valorisation and training of shop staff on sustainability issues). All reflect the expectations of the neo-consumer in the fashion sector.

In April 2014, another Copenhagen Fashion Summit provided very interesting requests to stakeholders, as defined by more than a hundred students participating in the Youth Fashion Summit 2014, in order to discuss the issues to be solved and solutions to be addressed around seven Rs. Here are the seven requests:

- *Resources.* 'We demand nothing but state reality: we "give 2 get".'
- *Rethink.* 'We demand that decision-makers rethink the role of a fashion designer.'
- *Re-arrange.* 'We demand you to be brave and stop business secrecy.'
- *Re-connect.* 'We demand world leaders to help us build a critical society.'
- *Reorganise.* 'We demand the industry to reorganise into collaborating competence clusters.'
- *Reach out.* 'We demand the industry, government and civil society to create a fashion democracy.'
- *Reliability.* 'We demand the fashion industry to enable us wearing experiences instead of garments.'

From the solutions provided, the need for a multi-stakeholder approach is evident: we will discuss this topic in the next chapter.

References and further reading

Bauman, Zigmunt (2002) *Modernità liquida* (Bari and Rome: Laterza).

—— (2010) *L'etica in un mondo di consumatori* (Bari and Rome: Laterza).

Botsman, Rachel, and Roo Rogers (2010) *What's Mine is Yours: The Rise of Collaborative Consumption* (New York: Harper Collins).

Campiglio, Emanuele (2012) *L'economia buona* (Milan: Bruno Mondadori).

Danish Fashion Institute and BSR (2012) *The NICE Consumer: Toward a Framework for Sustainable Fashion Consumption in the EU*, www.bsr. org/reports/BSR_NICE_Consumer_Discussion_Paper.pdf.

Fabris, Giampaolo (2008) *Societing* (Milan: Egea).

Fromm, Erich (1977) *Avere o essere?* (Milan: Mondadori).

Galimberti, Umberto (2009) *I miti del nostro tempo* (Milan: Feltrinelli).

Institut Français de la Mode (2009) *Mode et consommation responsable. Regards des consommateurs* (Paris: IFM).

Magatti, Mauro (ed.) (2011) *Verso nuovi modelli di business* (Milan: Bruno Mondadori).

Morace, Francesco (2007) *Società felici. La morte del marketing postmoderno e il ritorno dei grandi valori* (Milan: Scheiwiller).

—— (2008) *Consum-autori. Le generazioni come imprese creative* (Milan: Scheiwiller).

—— (2012) *I paradigmi del futuro. Lo scenario dei trend* (Busto Arsizio, Italy: Nomos).

Rinaldi, Francesca Romana (2011) 'Moda eco-sostenibile: opportunità e rischi', *Les Cahiers Fashion Marketing*, http://lescahiersfm.com/it/articoli/98-modaeco-sostenibile-di-francesca-rinaldi.html.

Roberts, Kevin (2005) *Lovemarks. Il futuro oltre i brands* (Milan: Mondadori).

Saviolo, Stefania, and Antonio Marazza (2012) *Lifestyle brand. Le marche che ispirano la nostra vita* (Milan: Rizzoli Etas).

Zorino, M. Romana (2006) *Il consumatore* (Padua, Italy: Cleup).

2

The new value proposition: from the logic of profit to shared value

> Shared value is not social responsibility, philanthropy, or even sustainability, but a new way to achieve economic success.
>
> Porter and Kramer (2006).

2.1 The 3P relational model: this is where it all started

In 1984, Edward Freeman pioneered stakeholder theory and for the first time 'stakeholder' became a key term which, compared with 'shareholder', aims to include all the people who might affect the attainment of corporate objectives or be affected in turn by corporate actions. *Stakeholder view* proposes a relational concept of a company that does not choose profit maximisation as its only objective priority—and therefore only takes shareholders' needs and interests into consideration—but one for which consideration of the interests of all stakeholders becomes an indispensable factor. Clarkson divides them into two macro-categories:

- *Primary stakeholders*, defined as groups that 'without their continuous participation, a firm's survival would be compromised' (Clarkson 1995), meaning suppliers, consumers, investors, workers, financial institutions, associations and communities.

- *Secondary stakeholders*, inessential for the survival of the firm but which affect and are affected by its activity, such as competitors, the media, public opinion, and public and political institutions.

Returning to the relational concept of management, Perrini and Tencati define CSR (Corporate Social Responsibility) as the 'innovation for corporate sustainability and for the stakeholder network in which this is inserted' and 'a crucial strategic positioning for corporate management' (Perrini and Tencati 2008). The durability of the business is linked to a dual ability: to attract the best resources to guarantee continuity and development for economic activities, and to meet the expectations of the various stakeholders, thereby constructing and strengthening relations based on mutual trust and support. Therefore, responsibility does not end with a utilitarian type of relationship but involves a proactive attitude in considering a wide range of actors, even those who at first sight may seem less crucial for the company as they are not directly involved in its economic activities.

This concept is well represented by the 3P model (Fig. 2.1), which summarises the three main dimensions (economic, social and environmental) considered by CSR:

- *Profit* indicates the economic dimension

- *People* indicates the social dimension

- *Planet* indicates the environmental dimension

The expression 'triple bottom line', coined in 1977 by the sustainability guru John Elkington (1997), summarises this approach. *Bottom*

Figure 2.1 **The 3P model: 'Profit, People, Planet'.**

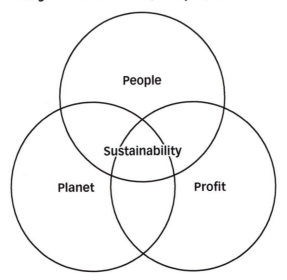

Source: Elkington (1997).

line translates as 'net income'; by adding the *triple* result, the author additionally considers environmental and social reporting. According to this perspective, in order to obtain growth in the long term, businesses need to incorporate into their management objectives that have an economic nature (the capacity to generate richness), an environmental nature (to ensure ecological balance) and a social nature (to guarantee social justice) (Pogutz 2007).

This approach is widely validated, as we shall see in this book, even within the fashion sector where there are also some specificities that make it particularly relevant, especially in the present competitive context.

The scarcity of theoretical contributions and models dealing with the sector's specific features gives rise to the need to create something tailor-made for the fashion industry that considers and clarifies the specific stakeholders with whom a responsible fashion company interacts, thereby establishing a relationship of mutual exchange (see Section 2.7).

2.2 Brief excursus on CSR (1950–90)

The first theoretical contributions on CSR addressed the issue mainly from the perspective of people, rather than from that of the company.[1]

Peter Drucker (1954) was the first to develop a definition of 'social responsibilities of business' which included social responsibility among the priority objectives of a company. In 1960, Keith Davis emphasised the influence of companies on society and assumed that there was a close link between social responsibility and power. Davis speaks of the 'iron law of responsibility' and says that if a company does not act in a socially responsible way, its power will deteriorate over time (Davis 1960). According to this perspective, therefore, incorporating the social dimension helps to bring about economic advantages in the long term.

Also in 1960, William Frederick investigated the topic of responsibility by claiming that a company's goal is the improvement of general social and economic conditions. Analysing the relationship between the business and the environmental context in which it is embedded, he underlines that companies have social duties towards the community: 'Enterprises have the obligation of working to improve society' (Frederick 1960).

In absolute contrast to these theories is Milton Friedman, winner of the Nobel Prize for economics in 1976 and promoter of a new liberalism. He claimed that if management also assumed social responsibilities (which differ from those requiring the creation of high profits and dividends), the foundations of free society would be undermined. In fact, the company's only social responsibility ought to be the maximisation of profit and investment recovery for shareholders. In his critique, Friedman (1970) defines as subversive any management that

---

1   In fact, Bowen, in his text *Social Responsibilities of the Businessman* (Bowen 1953), talks of social responsibility as the duty 'to pursue those policies, to make those decisions, or to follow those lines of action which are desirable in terms of the objectives and values of our society'.

Figure 2.2 **The CSR pyramid.**

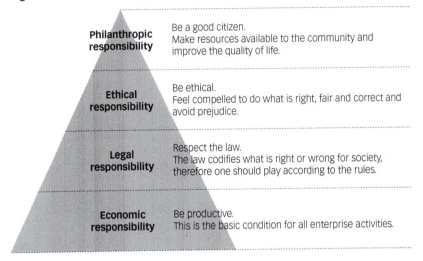

Source: Caroll (1991).

loses sight of the company's primary objective, profit, and 'accepts' social responsibilities.

In subsequent years, Archie Carroll (1991) divided the concept of responsibility into four hierarchical levels (Fig. 2.2):

- *Economic responsibility*: to obtain a positive economic result

- *Legal responsibility*: to comply with the law

- *Ethical responsibility*: to conform to social values and norms

- *Philanthropic responsibility*: to be a good citizen by making resources available to the community and contributing to a general improvement in quality of life

According to Carroll, philanthropic responsibilities, which include, for example, investments in favour of the territorial, social and cultural communities, are the only ones which are discretionary, or voluntary. Carroll introduces the concept of voluntarism as a CSR commitment, stating that every business can choose how it fulfils these different types of responsibility. However, only through the voluntary assumption of philanthropic responsibility can the company, as an economic institution, be considered 'a good corporate citizen', i.e. a subject able to match its own needs of survival and development with those of a more general nature.

2.3 The concept of sustainability adopted by institutions and the development of CSR

The first definition of sustainability accepted at a European level is that of sustainable development included in the Brundtland report[2] of 1987 and maintained by the UN's WCED (World Commission on Environment and Development): 'sustainable development [...] implies meeting the needs of the present without compromising the ability of future generations to meet their own needs.'[3]

From this definition it is clear that sustainable development implies, first, a concept that considers *future generations* to be involved in development, rather than just the present generation, and second, a *strategic* vision (long term) rather than a tactical (short term) vision.

Looking at the enterprise context, in the definition placed by the European Commission at the base of the social responsibility model, CSR is considered as 'the responsibility of enterprises for their impacts on society'. The Commission encourages that enterprises 'should have in place a process to integrate social, environmental, ethical human rights and consumer concerns into their business operations and core strategy in close collaboration with their stakeholders' (Commission of the European Communities 2011).

Since the end of the 1990s, the Commission's support for, and promotion of, the incorporation of CSR principles into corporate strategy

---

2   Named after the president of the Commission, the Norwegian Gro Harlem Brundtland.
3   www.un.org/documents/ga/res/42/ares42-187.htm.

has intensified, leading to the publication of two documents—the Green Paper[4] in 2001 and the White Paper[5] in 2005—introducing the guidelines for sustainable corporate behaviour.

According to the Green Paper, CSR can be considered as the 'voluntary integration of the social and ecological worries of enterprises for their activities and relations with the stakeholders'. The explanation goes on to say that 'being socially responsible means not only fulfilling legal expectations, but also beyond compliance and investing more into human capital, the environment, and the relations with stakeholders'.

2.3.1 The reasons for increasing interest in CSR

The reasons for increasing interest in CSR are common to a wide range of sectors and concern a number of changes which have taken place both in demand and supply:

- The awareness of the scarcity of our planet's resources

- The transformation of the consumer (see Chapter 1)

- The delocalisation of production and the globalisation of the supply chain

- The proliferation of scandals related to the use of child labour and the lack of compliance with the working conditions set down by the ILO (International Labour Organization), a specialist UN agency that pursues the promotion of social justice and of internationally acknowledged human rights, with particular reference to employment rights

- The increase in multi-stakeholder associations[6]

4   http://eur-lex.europa.eu/legal-content/EN/TXT/?uri=CELEX:
     52001DC0366.
5   www.community-wealth.org/sites/clone.community-wealth.org/files/
     downloads/report-european-commission.pdf.
6   For example, the Ethical Trading Initiative, the Fair Wear Foundation and
     the Worker Rights Consortium.

- The increased speed and low cost of information dissemination, thanks to computer technology, the Internet and social networks (Rancati 2007)

The result of all these factors is the growing importance of the concepts of traceability and transparency (as we shall see in detail in the following chapters). The latter is not only required by consumers but also by financial markets, and this is demonstrated by the creation of stock indexes like the Dow Jones Sustainability Indexes that only list companies that can show they meet certain environmental requirements. The desire to be included in these indexes has led to the development of social and ecological practices, especially among the big listed companies.

The Dow Jones Sustainability Indexes

Launched in 1999, the Dow Jones Sustainability Indexes are the first global indexes to monitor the financial performance of the main sustainability-driven companies. On the basis of collaboration between the Dow Jones Indexes and RobecoSAM,[7] they replicate the stock performance of companies that are world leaders in terms of economic, environmental and social requirements. Indexes are useful as a reference for investors wanting to incorporate sustainability considerations into their portfolios and constitute a platform which stimulates companies' commitment to adopt the best sustainable practices.

2.4 From shareholder value to shared value

When talking about sustainability in the fashion world it is necessary to start with a more general concept of responsibility: in fact,

---

7   RobecoSAM is an international investment company with a specific focus on sustainability investments: www.robecosam.com.

sustainability (economic, environmental and social) implies responsible behaviour, intended as the creation of value for stakeholders as well as for shareholders.

The word 'sustainability' would be meaningless without considering a new way of understanding value: in the past, 'creating value' in business simply meant making higher profits than the competition and dividends to distribute to those providing the capital. Something changed, especially following the financial crisis that began in 2008: the idea of 'shareholder value maximisation' in the short term is no longer sufficient and is radically changing into a concept that leads to the affirmation of new business models (Magatti 2011).

A chance to relaunch the market economy and get out of the crisis lies behind the appropriation by companies of what could be called 'context value'. This appears in different ways of paying greater attention to the environment, the social quality of the territory and the development of people, and which can in turn generate extra opportunities to create value.

In this new concept, sustainability is not considered a cost, but rather a competitive advantage that ought to be incorporated into a company's strategy.

The concept of value broadens to non-financial criteria and to a long-term temporal perspective, which are both summarised in the principle of valorisation of resources: valorising resources legitimises the company because it contributes directly to the wellbeing of all its stakeholders, be they near or far in space or time, internal or external to the business, starting with the company (consumers, employees, collaborators and suppliers) and the environment in general.

Porter and Kramer, in their article 'Creating Shared Value' published in the *Harvard Business Review* (2011), stated: 'The solution lies in the principle of shared value, which involves creating economic value in a way that *also* creates value for society by addressing its needs and challenges. Businesses must reconnect company success with social progress. Shared value is [...] a new way to achieve economic success.'

Figure 2.3 **Maslow's pyramid and Maslow's new pyramid in contextual logic.**

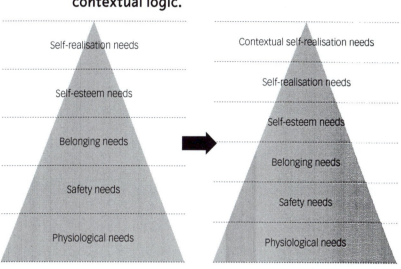

Source: Adapted from Maslow (1954).

Numerous texts on management which analyse the new business models come to the conclusion that the final step hypothesised by Maslow has now been taken: creating value means fulfilling the requirements of the levels above, which could be defined as 'contextual self-realisation needs' (Magatti 2011) (Fig. 2.3).

The other key element of shared value is the perspective of life-cycle assessment: with the gradual geographical dispersion of the company's activities it has become necessary to extend consideration to every link in the value chain and to the product's complete life-cycle.

Sustainability increases the chances of survival for firms in the medium to long term and represents a source of competitive advantage (*L'Impresa* 2009):

- *Improvement of risk management.* By adopting a strategy that is sensitive to the socio-environmental dimension, it is possible to reduce the sources of risk: reviewing internal processes prevents and limits the possible risks deriving from conduct that is not very responsible. The benefits can be observed in numerous fields, for example, job safety, disposal of highly polluting waste and the risk of possible boycotts.

- *Greater capacity to attract human capital, improvement of the business climate and of employee performance.* The greater capacity to motivate, involve and retain talent within one's company is a further positive contribution. With a corporate culture that increasingly encourages dialogue and transparency, comparison and co-operation become fundamental for the retention of current staff. These elements reflect positively on the ability to attract and retain clients as a faithful customers.

- *Increase in efficiency and optimisation of costs.* Structured CSR policies, in forcing internal processes to be reconsidered, promote improvements in efficiency and productivity. It is precisely through the process of organisational improvement within various roles that significant inefficiencies can be made good. Consider, for example, plans to reduce production waste or to re-use packaging materials.

- *Increase in capacity to attract financial resources.* A company which shows itself to be transparent and socially engaged establishes a climate of trust in its relations with institutions and financial markets, facilitating the collection of resources and access to credit. Furthermore, recent years have shown that financial analysts are increasingly appreciative of those companies that perform well even in the socio-environmental arena.

- *Reinforcing brand value.* By incorporating socio-environmental policies and ethical conduct, the company can build a legacy of intangible assets comprising values such as trust, security and loyalty, which in turn helps to strengthen its relationship with stakeholders.

The advantages in terms of image and reputation are part of the old ideas of CSR (Lazlo 2008) and sustainability: having abandoned the

Table 2.1 **Interpretation of sustainability.**

Interpretation	Main stakeholders considered	Requirements	Objectives
Cost	Shareholders	—	Maximisation of profit
Competitive advantage	Multi-stakeholder	Initiatives associated with the core business	Creation of value
Business	Multi-stakeholder in context	Initiatives attached to the core business Sustainable innovation	Creation of shared value

concept of sustainability as a cost, *sustainable innovation is the drive that transforms the interpretation of sustainability as a competitive advantage into the interpretation of sustainability as a business* (Table 2.1).

The innovation realised thanks to business models based on responsibility is based on the creation of shared value: the increase in value for shareholders will then be a direct consequence of the increase in value for all stakeholders. If this is an ideal world, then in reality many companies think about sustainability and CSR as a mere public relations tool aimed at strengthening their reputation (cost logic). Porter and Kramer (2006) argue that it is still the case for many companies that:

> CSR is seen as a public relations tool, rather than a value-creating process in its own right, whose goal is to assist manufacturing companies in achieving sustainability [...] some companies have claimed to pursue CSR, but in fact have only used contributions to social objectives as a mechanism for carrying on profit maximising operations. Profit is an integral part and a tangible way of evaluating a company's growth; however, it is not the only objective.

Sustainability's journey from cost logic to business logic is obligatory for creating shared value and provides at least two fundamental elements: *dialogue with a multiplicity of stakeholders* and *CSR initiatives connected to the core business.*

2.5. Documenting sustainability: sustainability reporting and codes of ethics

The need for tools which make it possible to appreciate companies' actions at a social and environmental level within the logic of shared value has prompted the development of many standards and voluntary certifications.

The sustainability report is an independent public document aimed at communicating the choices, activities, results obtained and future projects of the company for all categories of stakeholders. In order for it to be truthful and effective, it must be incorporated into the planning, control and accounting tools adopted by the organisation and contain appropriately identified quantitative and qualitative indicators. Third-party auditing may also be engaged to ensure its accuracy. The most widely used international standards for corporate sustainability (see Section 7.3.4) are:

- WRAP (Worldwide Responsible Apparel Production)

- SA8000 (Social Accountability 8000), created by Social Accountability International

- GOTS (Global Organic Textile Standard)

Environmental standards assess a company's environmental performance; the guidelines developed by various international organisations, including CEFIC (European Chemical Industry Council) and PERI (Public Environmental Reporting Initiative), provide for the drafting of quantitative summaries on the basis of indicators measuring: environmental management, environmental impact, environmental performance, environmental efficiency and potential effect.

The most widely used international standards for environmental sustainability are classified with the prefix ISO 14000, which identifies a set of rules established by the ISO (International Organization for Standardization). The most famous of these is ISO 14001, which establishes the requirements for an environmental management system.

The guidelines provided by the GRI (Global Reporting Initiative), now in its third generation (G3.1), represent the best known and most widely used standard for environmental and social sustainability.

Another document drawn up by companies with increasing frequency is a code of ethics, a charter of rights and moral duties to which all members of the company, from the senior management down to the employees (and even suppliers), are subject. Its structure, by virtue of the absence of regulatory laws, is quite varied; in general, the document lists the ethical principles on which a business mission is based, the ethical norms to be followed when dealing with various stakeholders, the ethical standards of reference (for example, equity, transparency, honesty, fairness, protection of the environment and protection of health), and the internal sanctions provided for code infringements. Once it has decided to draw up a code of ethics, the company prepares it not only through discussion with those involved, but also by consulting all stakeholders on the sharing of moral principles. In addition, the company informs all workers about the code by means of specific ethical training activities.

The code of ethics can be associated with the code of conduct by highlighting a set of principles, commitments and ethical responsibilities that constitute the foundation of the company's activities (see Section 7.3.2). A typical code of conduct is that of Monnalisa, a company which for years has demonstrated a philosophy of extreme transparency and commitment towards environmental and social protection. Monnalisa SpA is a leading Italian children's clothing and accessories business. It is positioned at the high end of the market, and is present in over 50 countries with selective distribution through flagship stores, shop-in-shops and franchises in the most exclusive department stores and boutiques of the world. An extract from its code of conduct for suppliers is shown below.

Code of conduct for Monnalisa suppliers

In Monnalisa we are committed to:

- A quality, trendy product with a strong identity, together with flexible, reliable and personalised service
- A dynamic and challenging work environment compliant with the rights and dignity of individuals
- Appropriate and responsible conduct for all our operations
- A fruitful and sustainable relationship with suppliers, customers and partners
- Respect for the environment and care for one's own territory

In accordance with the values of our company, we expect the same commitment from all our manufacturers. It is necessary, therefore, to comply with the following minimum standards.

Workers

Child labour. Child labour cannot be employed, so the supplier commits not to hire minors and not to make use of them directly or indirectly. Only workers over the age of 15 or over the age established for compulsory education can be recruited. Children excluded from work should be guaranteed adequate economic assistance and training opportunities.

Forced and compulsory labour. The supplier does not support, favour, make available, directly or indirectly, forced or compulsory labour and does not require staff to deliver cash deposits or identity cards as part of an employment contract; does not support or resort to human trafficking, either directly or indirectly through entities that provide labour to the company.

Coercion and harassment. The supplier ensures dignified and respectful treatment of staff; therefore, any behaviour involving the use of corporal punishment, mental or physical coercion, verbal abuse, sexual harassment, or rigid or brutal attitudes is not tolerated.

→

Freedom of association and right to collective bargaining. The supplier ensures compliance with choices made by employees on the right to associate, to join trade unions and take part in collective bargaining, and manages relations with its own staff in compliance with the National Collective Agreement for the sector to which it belongs, if one exists. Non-discrimination against any employee representative is guaranteed.

Non-discrimination. Discrimination at work is prohibited. The supplier guarantees equal opportunities and treatment regardless of race, colour, gender, religion, political opinion, nationality, social origin or other characteristics. Out of respect for the person and for the principles of confidentiality, it does not interfere with the choices or views of its employees.

Disciplinary practices. Any use of disciplinary practices is conducted in accordance with what is provided by the National Collective Agreement of reference and in any case respecting the physical, mental, emotional and moral integrity of the worker.

Working hours. Working hours must comply with applicable legislation and employment contracts. When not determined by legislation, the number of working hours must not exceed 48 per week plus 12 hours overtime. Overtime is voluntary, should not be routinely requested and must be compensated by a salary supplement. Furthermore, except under extraordinary circumstances, employees are entitled to at least one day of rest every seven days.

Pay. Salaries and wages paid by the supplier to its employees comply, insofar as the contractual minimum, with the salary tables provided by the Collective Agreement of reference. No deduction from salary or wage shall be applied for disciplinary reasons.

Working environment. Working conditions must be dignified. The supplier guarantees a hygienic and healthy environment, promoting the best health and safety conditions, and bearing in mind the most up-to-date knowledge and the specific risks of the sector.

→

Environment

In production activities, it shall be necessary to minimise adverse effects on the environment and natural resources, simultaneously protecting the health and safety of the end-consumer and observing all applicable environmental laws and regulations.

Product safety

Monnalisa does not produce or import chemical substances (in themselves or as components of compounds or other items) but, nevertheless, as a user of such substances it has an interest and needs to receive information from its suppliers to ensure that the materials processed by Monnalisa are:

- Compliant with REACH (Registration, Evaluation, Authorization and Restriction of Chemicals) regulations, and with EC regulations on chemical substances, their control and their safe use

- Free of SVHC (Substance of Very High Concern) or containing less than 0.1% (w/w).[8]

Handling confidential information

The supplier commits not to disclose to any person, firm or company and shall ensure that its employees do not disclose to these third parties, either directly or indirectly, technical know-how or other confidential information—including by way of example and not limited to, all data, drawings, designs, sketches, specifications, samples or models used to manufacture the products—which it may acquire in relation to the execution of this contract.

Upon expiration, termination or cancellation of this contract, the supplier shall return to Monnalisa, immediately and without retaining copies, every document, drawing, design, model, prototype or other device containing information specific to the structural characteristics or functionalily of the manufacturing process that it has obtained in view of the implementation of this agreement. As a fulfilment of the

---

8   weight/weight, i.e. the weight of SVHC in the weight of any product.

→

obligation, the supplier commits to ensure that restitution is made also by all its employees, suppliers and collaborators.

Other laws

The supplier commits to observe all applicable laws and regulations, including those relative to manufacturing, pricing, selling and distribution of goods, including codes, rules and local and national regulations, treaties and voluntary standards for the relevant sector.

Control and verification

- The supplier commits to accept inspection visits by second parties (carried out for and on behalf of Monnalisa SpA) and to make available to the evaluators/consultants any documents that may be required to verify the correct implementation of SA8000 and this code of conduct.

- Monnalisa reserves the right to terminate any business with suppliers that seriously or deliberately infringe the supplier code of conduct or make use of subcontractors that seriously or deliberately infringe the code.

- The terms of this supplier code of conduct are an integral part of the commercial agreements that must be complied with by the supplier.

Supplier commitment

The supplier confirms that they have read and understood the code of conduct, commits to take positive action towards the implementation of the code of conduct and to observe the code in respect of all employees and workers, through clear verbal information and displaying the text in a visible place accessible to everyone.

Source: http://portal.monnalisa.eu/about_the_group_en/social_responsibility/suppliers__code_of_ethical_conduct.aspx.

The Camera Nazionale della Moda Italiana [National Chamber for Italian Fashion] has also decided to establish clear guidelines on sustainability. The *Manifesto della sostenibilità per la moda italiana* [sustainability manifesto for Italian fashion][9] can be considered a code of conduct for the associated companies, and defines their commitments with the following terms:

- *Design*. The sustainable fashion company designs long-lasting quality products which minimise the impact on ecosystems.

- *Choice of raw materials*. The sustainable fashion company uses raw materials, materials and fabrics with a high environmental and social value.

- *Processing of raw materials and production*. The sustainable fashion company reduces the environmental and social impacts of its activities and recognises the contribution of each one to the value of the product.

- *Distribution, marketing and sales*. The sustainable fashion company includes sustainability criteria along the entire route that the product takes to the customer.

- *Management systems*. The sustainable fashion company engages in the continuous improvement of the company's performance.

- *Country system*. The sustainable fashion company supports the territory and 'Made in Italy'.

- *Corporate ethics*. The sustainable fashion company incorporates universal values in its trademark.

- *Transparency*. The sustainable fashion company communicates its commitment to sustainability to its stakeholders in a transparent manner.

9   www.cameramoda.it/file/it/Manifesto.pdf.

- *Education*. The sustainable fashion company promotes ethics and sustainability to consumers and everyone else with whom it comes into contact.

2.6 CSR in the fashion world and dimensions of responsibility

In 2009, Dickson *et al.* proposed a new model of social responsibility for the T&A (textile and apparel) industry. Their model shows the different results that can arise from a three-way approach to the environment, people and systems by adopting a philosophy and implementing actions that go in the direction of ethics and of economy (Fig. 2.4). According to the authors, in order for a company in the T&A sector to be considered responsible, it needs to be motivated

Figure 2.4 **The model of social responsibility for the T&A sector according to Dickson *et al.***

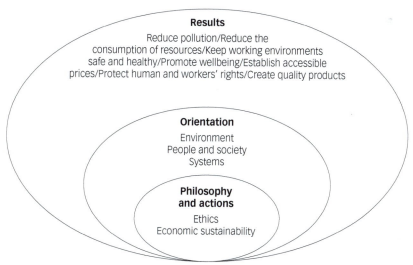

Results
Reduce pollution/Reduce the consumption of resources/Keep working environments safe and healthy/Promote wellbeing/Establish accessible prices/Protect human and workers' rights/Create quality products

Orientation
Environment
People and society
Systems

Philosophy and actions
Ethics
Economic sustainability

Source: Dickson *et al.* (2009).

by a philosophy that balances ethics and profit and to consider its social responsibility in everyday decisions; it must adopt an approach aimed at a systematic assessment of environmental and social sustainability; and it must constantly strive towards improvement and to the reduction of socio-environmental impact at a global level. The areas in which companies must focus more to improve their results are represented by: safety, product quality, wellbeing and safety of workers, reduction of pollution and of the consumption of natural resources, consumer welfare, price level and respect for human rights.

Returning to aspects of the 'triple bottom line' theory, Dickson *et al.* simultaneously consider performance at the financial, environmental

Figure 2.5 **Dickson *et al.*'s extended model.**

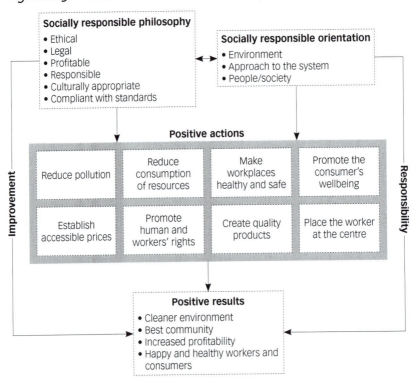

Source: Dickson *et al.* (2009).

and social levels. In this way, their model assesses the *entire life-cycle of a product* (from the provision of raw materials up to the moment at which the product is discarded) and the network of *all stakeholders*.

In the extended version of the model (Fig. 2.5), the *worker-centric orientation* of the CSR is reinforced. To adopt a worker-centric orientation means 'to act in culturally appropriate and internationally informed ways' (Dickson *et al.* 2009). It is not sufficient, therefore, to understand and comply with the rules and local customs of the countries in which the manufacturing factories are located: it is necessary to go further and also take account of the workers' expectations.

Another element is the *dynamic perspective*: the social responsibility of fashion companies is not static, but is affected by continuity of effort, both in terms of actions and in obtaining results.

2.7 A new model of responsibility in fashion

If, on the one hand, the attention placed by the Dickson *et al.* model on a worker-centric orientation for CSR is valuable, on the other hand it is essential that companies answer the needs of all stakeholders: a *worker-centric* concept which works towards the creation of a true partnership with suppliers must also be incorporated into a *consumer-centric* concept in order to give weight to issues like transparency and traceability, which are becoming increasingly important for the neo-consumer.

As stated in the Introduction, this book aims to present a new management model based on three variables that fashion companies need to manage better in the short and long term:

- Ethics

- Aesthetics

- Economic efficiency

Table 2.2 **New model for responsibility in fashion: the stakeholders and the dimensions of context.**

Dimension of context	Stakeholder of reference	Main demands
Environmental	Environment	• How to reduce environmental impact?
Social	Social territory, workers and consumers	• How to contribute to the economic development of the territory (district, region, nation) in which the company is present? • How to respect the rights of workers and develop their competences? • How to respect consumers?
Media	Media	• How to interact with stakeholders through the media?
Artistic, cultural and territorial	Art, culture and territory	• How to give back to culture as the main source of inspiration in terms of aesthetic codes? • How to give back to the landscape?
Regulatory and institutional	Institutions	• How to behave responsibly, respecting regulations and being transparent towards institutions?
Ethics	All stakeholders	• What is the right compensation for all stakeholders? • What are the codes of conduct to respect human dignity and respect the consumer? • What are the codes of conduct to safeguard the planet's resources? • How can a balanced relationship be established with the social actors of reference? • How is it possible to contribute to the social and civil progress of the collectivities and communities of reference, be they local or global? • How can aesthetics be a bearer of morality and positive values?

The three variables connect the fashion company with different contexts: those of environmental, social and economic efficiency are common to many other sectors. Other contexts are added to fashion which characterise the sector itself: media; artistic, cultural and territorial; regulatory and institutional; and ethical value (Table 2.2, Fig. 2.6).

Figure 2.6 **New model for responsibility in fashion: the stakeholders.**

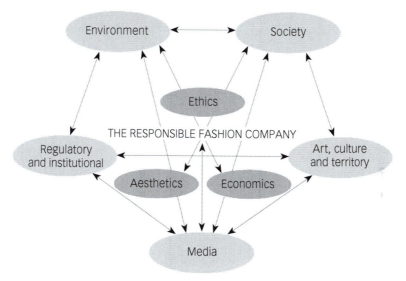

2.7.1 Environmental dimension

The environmental dimension refers to the 'environmental' stakeholder and concerns all the actions that the company can take to reduce environmental impact.

Referring to interchange and balance with the environment means working to reduce the environmental impact generated by every production activity. For fashion companies, therefore, examples of this include carbon dioxide emissions during production activities, the use of water to process raw materials, and the use and disposal of chemicals in the production process. Chapter 3 presents an overview of different types of action directed towards this goal and outlines various company case histories.

2.7.2 Social dimension

The social dimension refers to the stakeholders of 'social territory, workers and consumers', and covers all the actions that fashion companies can take to contribute towards workers' rights and the development of their skills, respect for consumers, and the valorisation of the territory's social resources.

Given the globalisation and localisation processes taking place, the responsible fashion company tries to protect the rights of workers and develop their skills in all countries in which production, logistics and distribution take place. The guarantee of quality, safety and transparency represents a mark of respect for the consumer. The responsible fashion company can contribute to the social, cultural, economic and aesthetic progress of the firm, proving itself to be the agent of its own change. Chapter 4 presents an overview of different types of actions directed towards this goal, and describes different company case histories.

2.7.3 Media dimension

The media dimension refers to 'media' stakeholders and concerns all the actions that the fashion company can take to improve communication with every stakeholder and with public opinion in general. The way one communicates is a tool to affirm one's identity and to spread one's manifesto of values, which includes ethics. Regardless of their positioning, fashion companies today face a great challenge, namely that of communicating directly with the consumer in a one-to-one exchange, rather than solely in a one-to-many exchange, as with traditional channels. The authenticity of the relationship is the new mantra. Chapter 5 presents an overview of the different types of actions directed towards this goal by describing different business case histories.

2.7.4 Artistic, cultural and territorial dimension

The artistic, cultural and territorial dimension refers to 'art, culture and territory' stakeholders, and concerns all the actions that the fashion company can take to give something back to the landscape and culture, which are the main sources of inspiration, resources and competences associated with creative and productive processes.

Historically fashion, an élite industry, has always benefited from strong associations with art and culture (consider, for example, Chanel, Dior and Versace, among others), because it proposes aesthetic content equipped with an artistic component—pieces of art for daily use. Furthermore, clothes and accessories offer aesthetic elements which are not only the result of inspiration and creativity, but which aspire to express a sense of socio-cultural change: the emancipation of women with the Chanel image, the new Armani female 'working outfit', or the conceptual look of Prada's contemporary women. The aesthetic component of the garment is intrinsically associated with the evolution of society, and often the artist—and the creative designer—understand this better than the business manager, who often looks more to the past than to the present or future. Therefore, the recovery of an organic and concrete relationship with the world of art and culture has much to do with the added aesthetic value which, in turn, is an essential part of the value proposition in fashion.

The *genius loci* and the characteristics of the landscape in which the company is located are also important sources of aesthetic inspiration: the responsible fashion company is compelled to give something back to the place that constitutes its cultural *humus*, from which it drew during the creative phase.

The film industry is another artistic field to have inspired many fashion companies and offers designers a sounding board for the representation of character and clothing archetypes.

Chapter 6 presents an overview of different types of actions directed towards this goal, describing different case studies.

2.7.5 Regulatory and institutional dimension

No textile manufacturing process, from spinning to ennobling, comes within the scope of various national or regional laws on organic farming. Because of this legislative gap, the GOTS (Global Organic Textile

Standard) has been developed and adopted internationally, introducing environmental and social criteria to be applied to the textile manufacturing system. This ethical and environmental certification is therefore a guarantee for the consumer.

Chapter 7 shows an overview of different types of actions directed towards this goal.

2.7.6 Ethical value dimension

The dimension of ethical value connects the company with all its stakeholders and concerns every action that the fashion company can take to ensure appropriate compensation for each stakeholder: for example, implementing codes of conduct relating to respect for human dignity and for the consumer, safeguarding the resources of the planet, establishing a balanced relationship with all the social actors of reference and offering a contribution to the social and civil progress of the collectivities and communities of reference, be they local or global. Compared to the previous dimensions, ethical values in the fashion world are placed on a different and superior level: it makes sense to speak of ethics with reference to the economic, environmental, political, artistic, cultural and legislative-institutional contexts.

In Chapter 9 the role of ethics is illustrated as a prerequisite for the achievement of long-term balance between the company and its social and environmental context.

2.8 'Food for thought': a comparison of responsibilities in the T&A and food sectors

In recent years, new critical success factors have been imposed that are common to both food and T&A sectors: the main one is represented *by a new partnership with suppliers to ensure quality, transparency of the value chain and traceability of the product.* The partnership with suppliers (intended as a relationship of trust, long-term contracts and early investment) can also be useful for communicating product differentiation, by using a different narrative for small producers compared to large-scale distribution.[10] T&A and food can be associated in a number of ways:[11]

- The agricultural origin of the raw material. Cotton, hemp and flax are classified as agricultural products. In addition to food, T&A's connection with other non-food sectors is most tangible, at least for Italian companies, with regard to cosmetics: natural and organic cosmetics allow the valorisation of agricultural products such as honey, propolis, citrus fruit and bergamot (essential oils), lavender and other officinal herbs.

- As in fashion, the food industry's supply chain has experienced intense internationalisation over the last few years, with large food companies moving production to developing countries. For this reason, the values of environmental and social sustainability are becoming increasingly important: organic certification, Fairtrade and SA8000 all help towards reducing unfair competition between countries with different legislative guarantees.

- As sustainability is influenced by fluctuations in price (of raw materials/food), projects to regulate a fair market are also being introduced in the Western world by defining conditions of guarantee and protection that are able to support rural production areas that would otherwise not be covered (for example, consortia, production co-operatives, and projects with a higher remuneration than the market average).

10   In the case of small producers, quality and transparency are often emphasised from an emotional point of view, giving an account of what is behind the product and, even, highlighting the supplier. Product history is not generally emphasised in large-scale distribution, which instead focuses on the safety and standardisation of the product itself, long-term supply relationships and the reliability of the distribution chain.

11   Interview with Alessandro Pulga, director of the ICEA (Italian Institute for Ethical and Environmental Certification).

- Safety is an increasingly important factor and is considered in a very different way by different stakeholders. Pesticides and chemical additives are an important tool for increasing productivity in the fields; however, it is crucial for the health and safety of consumers to protect against and prevent side-effects and illnesses resulting from ingestion and skin contact with these substances.

However, some elements distinguish the two sectors:

- The presence of stricter rules on food and its labelling (see Chapter 7). In the European Union, the food industry is one of the most standardised at a general level. Europe produced the first law to regulate the organic production of agricultural products. EEC regulation 2092/91 was the first harmonisation standard at a European community level; the regulation of DOC and PDO production followed a few years later.[12] Organic food has benefited from this legislation to provide certainty for markets, trading, consumers and public authorities. This does not occur in other sectors, such as T&A and cosmetics, which do not have a law regulating the use of the term 'organic': this is why voluntary certification is very important in these sectors.

- The greater importance of health and safety, deriving from the different ways a product is used: worn in the case of fashion, ingested in the case of food. Attention to safety is greater within the food industry as non-compliance with minimum safety standards has a much more immediate effect, as seen in the cases of excessive methanol content in wine, or with BSE (Bovine Spongiform Encephalopathy) or dioxin contamination elsewhere. In other sectors these standards are less stringent because they do not directly affect people's health.

12　'Denominazione di Origine Controllata' [controlled designation of origin] and 'Protected Designation of Origin', both certifying that a food product has been produced within the specified region using defined methods and that it satisfies a defined quality standard.

Sustainability is one of the main trends characterising the agricultural food sector over the last decade. According to Alessandro Pulga, director of ICEA, there are various reasons for this:

- Italy's rediscovery of products that characterise Italian cuisine and the Mediterranean diet in general, which have gone on to be popular all over the world.

- The rapid growth of organic farming and the market consolidation of 'green' agricultural products, as shown by the introduction of branded lines by the main large-scale organised distribution chains.

- The recent interest in corporate responsibility and fair trade also shown by the large-scale distributors.

- The development of ethical purchasing groups.

- The measurement and reduction of carbon footprint and of the overall environmental impact of production processes.

> Responsibility in the food sector means responding to these trends and guaranteeing a quality product at a sustainable price: unfortunately, some scandals occurred some years ago in the food sector like BSE, a disease universally known as 'mad cow disease', dioxin in chickens, etc., and this has attracted everyone's attention to values of product safety and traceability. Requirements that should be implicit and taken for granted have become points of marketing value and even subject to voluntary certification. Selling safety means wasting time and not making progress. The hygienic and sanitary safety of products should be something that is taken for granted, while the true values to invest in are environmental and social sustainability (Alessandro Pulga).

The agricultural food sector can be considered an example of best practice in corporate responsibility for various reasons, especially: the widespread development of environmental sustainability; the creation of many associations for the protection of consumer rights (including

Slow Food); and the presence of many companies (new or established) successfully implementing all the principles of responsibility. One example is illycaffè, which has adapted a responsible fashion enterprise model as described in one of the case studies which follow.

In Italy, there are some perfect examples of these crucial new factors for success: Slow Food and Terra Madre particularly represent best practice especially in terms of marketing and communication.

Slow Food and Terra Madre for good, clean and fair food

Slow Food is an international nonprofit association. In 2012 it numbered 100,000 members, volunteers and supporters in 150 countries, 1,500 *condotte* (local offices), and a network of 2,000 communities practising sustainable, quality food production on a small scale. Founded in 1986 by Carlo Petrini, Slow Food aims to promote the interests associated with food as a bearer of pleasure, culture, traditions, identity and lifestyle, not to mention sustenance, respectful of territory and local tradition.

The Slow Food motto is 'good, clean and fair' (Fig. 2.7), three adjectives that define the elementary characteristics of food: 'good' not only relative to the sense of pleasure associated with its qualities of taste and smell, but also to the complex sphere of feelings, memories and implications of identity arising from the sentimental value of food; 'clean', which means a product in keeping with ecosystems and the environment; 'fair', compliant with the concepts of social justice in terms of production and marketing.

Through its network of people who are active on the local, national and international stage, Slow Food:

- Co-ordinates and carries out projects that research, catalogue and promote the protection of food biodiversity.

- Promotes initiatives for the development of eco-friendly agriculture.

- Preserves and valorises the historical and cultural identity of the specific territory associated with a particular production process,

→

Figure 2.7 **The manifesto of quality according to Slow Food.**

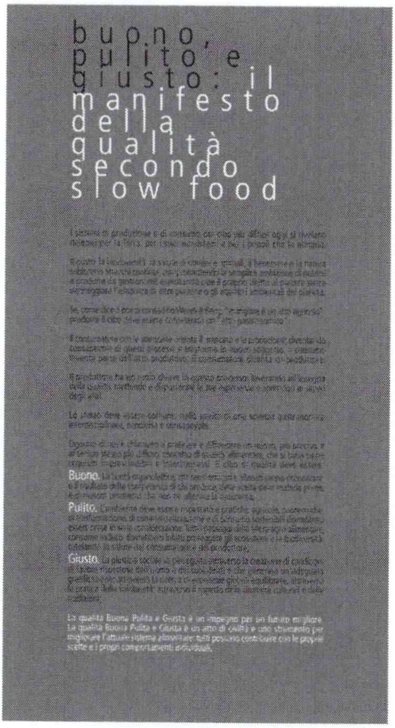

Source: www.slowfood.it/filemanager/SF_ITALIA/pdf/ManifestoBuonoPulitoGiusto.pdf.

mainly through the establishment of 'Praesidia' to protect biodiversity.

- Develops relations, activities and initiatives with and between food communities, comprising all those who work in the production and food processing sector.

- Favours a reduction of the distribution chain, and a direct relationship between producer/co-producer and the organisation of food and wine tourism activities.

- Promotes, organises, manages and participates in educational activities at both school and university level through research, co-ordination, training and modernisation projects, and plans and arranges programmes related to food and sensory culture.

Slow Food and its founder Carlo Petrini are connected to the international Terra Madre network, made up of all those who want to act to preserve, encourage and promote methods of sustainable food production in harmony with nature, the landscape and tradition.

Through the sale of its products in the global marketplace, Terra Madre's vision opposes random development and the quest for systematic and constant increases in profit and margins. In fact, the relentless drive for profit causes very serious repercussions for all of us, as taxpayers and inhabitants of the planet. However, it's the small producers who are first to pay the price for these mechanisms because they do not have the means to access local commercial channels and are crushed by subsidy systems that do not create a level playing field for developing agricultural activity.

Source: Interview with Piero Sardo, president of the Slow Food Foundation for Biodiversity.

illycaffè: differentiation and responsibility in the value chain

illycaffè was founded by Francesco Illy in 1993. Its mission is to 'produce high quality coffee and be a responsible company, based on the values that have inspired the company for over 75 years'.

If we ask Andrea Illy, the current president of the company, why illycaffè can be considered a responsible company, his answer is this: 'illycaffè chose to be a stakeholder company: its priority is no longer that of the shareholder, but that of all the stakeholders.' The illycaffè stakeholders, on the other hand, assume a precise hierarchy (Fig. 2.8). 'illycaffè,' says Andrea Illy, 'has decided to pursue a three-way approach to sustainability: economic, social and environmental.'

Economic sustainability

Economic balance is guaranteed through the creation of value shared equitably among all stakeholders. illycaffè promotes economic sustainability by creating value for everyone it deals with: consumers buy quality products at the best quality/price ratio; clients generate better

→

Figure 2.8 **Hierarchy of illycaffè stakeholders.**

Consumers

Clients

Workers

Suppliers

Community*

Shareholders

* In a broader sense, including the state, the local community, customers and suppliers.

profits and margins; employees are immersed in an environment which offers safety and serene and favourable working conditions; suppliers enjoy, on average, greater margins and lower risk in the long term; the community develops thanks to the satellite industries that the company promotes and the taxes that it pays; and as a result, the shareholders see the value of the company grow.

Social sustainability

Growth (social and individual) is pursued through knowledge. The objective is to put all stakeholders in a position to be trained in order to make their economic activity more profitable. For this reason illycaffè decided to create the University of Coffee with courses for suppliers, dealers and consumers. More than 85,000 people (over 21,000 in 2011 alone) have attended these courses in 12 years. Thanks to the University of Coffee, operators' margins and the quality of suppliers are both increasing. The company supports and creates sustainability at a social level by stimulating the concept of growth: consumers, thanks to their direct experience with illycaffè, deepen their awareness

→

of coffee culture and become 'connoisseurs'; customers serving illy-caffè can develop their own knowledge and, thus, their professional reputation; collaborators are offered opportunities for self-fulfilment, development of skills and professional growth; benefits for suppliers derive from reputation and the acquisition of know-how and, in the case of the raw material manufacturers, their living conditions improve as a result; the community in which the company operates enjoys the reflection of visibility and image; and shareholders collect the fruits of this virtuous circle in terms of reputation and authority.

Environmental sustainability

Environmental balance is pursued through respect for the environment expressed by the threefold imperative: 'whenever possible, no pollution, no waste, use renewable raw materials'. illycaffè promotes respect for the environment, actively involving all its stakeholders: it offers recyclable packaging to customers and consumers; a pleasant working environment and the utmost attention to safety for employees; to raw material suppliers it teaches agronomic practices that respect the ecosystem; it guarantees an ecologically advanced and certified industrial site to the community; and shareholders, as a result, are guaranteed maximum control of environmental risk.

The behaviour, consumption and lifestyle of all human beings have an impact that is, progressively, increasingly relevant to the natural, social and economic balance of our planet. As a result, the fundamental awareness and commitment of each and every one of us to respect and defend the world in which we live is becoming more important.

Sustainability is therefore a movement of thoughts and actions with the objective of seeking a balance between the legitimate achievements of modernity and the possibility that those who come after us will have at least the same opportunities. On the other hand, the market economy is based on trust. For this, citizens and consumers are increasingly attentive to the reputation of the companies and brands with which they enter into a relationship. A good reputation means being rigorous and transparent, avoiding any form of injustice—from

→

Figure 2.9 **Coffee harvesting in Ethiopia.**

© Courtesy of Elisabetta Illy.

exploitation to conflicts of interests—and promoting business practices that are sustainable from an environmental, social and economic
point of view.

In the light of all this, ethics, together with quality, is the basic value
for illycaffè, adhering in real terms to the idea of sustainability through
its behaviour and its products by adopting advanced technologies in
order to continue offering the consumer the best possible quality.

Source: Interview with Andrea Illy, president and managing director of illycaffè.

References and further reading

Allwood, Julian M., Søren Ellebaek Laursen, Cecilia Malvido de Rodríguez and Nancy M.P. Bocken (2006) *Well Dressed?* (Cambridge, UK: University of Cambridge Institute of Manufacturing).

Arvidsson, Adam, and Nicolai Peitersen (2011) *The Ethical Economy* (New York, Columbia University Press).

Bowen, Howard R. (1953) *Social Responsibilities of the Businessman* (New York: Harper).

Bowie, Norman E. (1999) *Business Ethics: A Kantian Perspective* (Oxford, UK: Blackwell).

Carroll, Archie B. (1991) 'The Pyramid of Corporate Social Responsibility: Toward the Moral Management of Organization Stakeholders', *Business Horizons* 34.4: 39-48.

Clarkson, Max B. (1995) 'A Stakeholder Framework for Analyzing and Evaluating Corporate Social Responsibility', *Academic of Management Review* 20.1: 92-117.

Coda, Vittorio (1995) *L'orientamento strategico dell'impresa* (Turin: Utet).

Commission of the European Communities (2001) *Green Paper. Promoting a European Framework for Corporate Social Responsibility*, www.csr-in-commerce.eu/data/files/resources/717/com_2001_0366_en.pdf.

—— (2011) *Communication from the Commission to the European Parliament, the Council, the European Economic and Social Committee and the Committee of the Regions: A renewed EU strategy 2011–14 for Corporate Social Responsibility*, http://eur-lex.europa.eu/LexUriServ/LexUriServ.do?uri=COM:2011:0681:FIN:EN:PDF.

Davis, Keith (1960) 'Can Business Afford to Ignore Social Responsibilities?', *California Management Review* 2.3: 70-6.

Dickson, Marsha A., Suzanne Loker and Molly Eckman (2009) *Social Responsibility in the Global Apparel Industry* (New York: Fairchild Books).

Drucker, Peter F. (1954) *The Practice of Management* (New York: Harper).

Elkington, John (1994) 'Towards the Sustainable Corporation: Win-win-win Business Strategies for Sustainable Development', *California Management Review*, 36.2: 90-100.

—— (1997) *Cannibals with Forks: The Triple Bottom Line of 21st Century Business* (Oxford, UK: Capstone Publishing).

Fletcher, Kate (2008) *Sustainable Fashion and Textiles: Design Journeys* (London: Earthscan).

Frederick, William C. (1960) 'The Growing Concern Over Business Responsibility', *California Management Review* 2.4: 54-61.

Freeman, R. Edward (1984) *Strategic Management: A Stakeholder Approach* (Boston, MA: Pitman).

Friedman, Milton (1970) 'The Social Responsibility of Business Is To Increase Its Profits', *The New York Times Magazine*, 13 September: 32-3, 122-6.

Grant, Robert (2008) *Contemporary Strategy Analysis. Sixth Edition* (Oxford, UK: Blackwell).

L'Impresa (2009), 'Verso una governance sostenibile', *L'Impresa* 4/2009: 25-7.

Institut Français de la Mode (2009) *Mode et consommation responsable. Regards des consommateurs* (Paris: IFM).

Latouche, Serge (2008) *Breve trattato sulla decrescita serena* (Turin: Bollati Boringhieri).

Lazlo, Chris (2008) *Sustainable Value: How the World's Leading Companies Are Doing Well by Doing Good* (Stanford, CA: Stanford Business Books).

Lunghi, Carla, and Eugenia Montagni (2007) *La moda della responsabilità* (Milan: Franco Angeli).

Magatti, Mauro (ed.) (2011) *Verso nuovi modelli di business* (Milan: Bruno Mondadori).

Masini, Carlo (1970) *Lavoro e risparmio* (Turin: Utet).

Maslow, Abraham H. (1954) *Motivazione e personalità* (Rome: Armando, 1992).

McDonough, William, and Michael Braungart (2002) *Cradle to Cradle: Remaking the Way We Make Things* (New York: North Point Press).

Meadows, Donella H., Dennis L. Meadows, Jorgen Randers and William W. Behrens (1972) *The Limits to Growth* (London: Universe Books).

Mora, Emanuela (2009) *Fare moda. Esperienze di produzione e consumo* (Milan: Bruno Mondadori).

Nussbaum, Martha C. (2012) *Not for Profit: Why Democracy Needs the Humanities* (Princeton, NJ: Princeton University Press).

Perrini, Francesco, and Antonio Tencati (2008) *Corporate Social Responsibility: Un nuovo approccio strategico alla gestione d'impresa* (Milan: Egea).

Pieraccini, Silvia (2009) 'Eco-moda: all'etica si aggiunge la bellezza', *Il Sole 24 Ore*, 18 April.

Pogutz, Stefano (2007) 'Responsabilità sociale d'impresa e pratica aziendale: una rassegna delle principali esperienze', in Romano Benini (ed.), *L'impresa responsabile e la comunità intraprendente. Responsabilità sociale, territorio e piccolo imprese in rete* (Avellino, Italy: Halley).

—— (2008) 'Sustainable Development, Corporate Sustainability and Corporate Social Responsibility: The Missing Link', in Peter Utting and Jennifer Clapp (eds.), *Taming Corporate Capitalism: New Perspectives on Business Regulation and Sustainable Development* (Oxford, UK: Oxford University Press).

Porter, Michael E. (1985) *Competitive Advantage: Creating and Sustaining Superior Performance* (New York: The Free Press).

Porter, Michael E., and Mark R. Kramer (2006) 'Strategy and Society: The Link Between Competitive Advantage and Corporate Social Responsibility', *Harvard Business Review* 84.12.

—— (2011) 'Creating Shared Value', *Harvard Business Review* 89.1–2.

Rancati, Elisa (2007) 'Il tempo nelle imprese orientate alla concorrenza', in Silvio M. Brondoni (ed.). *Market-driven management e mercati globali* (Turin: Giappichelli).

Testoni, Luca (2010) *L'ultima sfilata. Processo alla casta della moda italiana* (Milan: Sperling & Kupfer).

Valdani, Enrico (2003) *Marketing strategico. Un'impresa proattiva per sviluppare capacità market driving e valore* (Milan: Etas).

3
Fashion and the environment

Man is both creature and moulder of his environment, which gives him physical sustenance and affords him the opportunity for intellectual, moral, social and spiritual growth. In the long and tortuous evolution of the human race on this planet a stage has been reached when, through the rapid acceleration of science and technology, man has acquired the power to transform his environment in countless ways and on an unprecedented scale. Both aspects of man's environment, the natural and the man-made, are essential to his well-being and to the enjoyment of basic human rights the right to life itself.

Stockholm Declaration on the
Human Environment (1972), art. 1.

3.1 The relationship between fashion and the environment

Definitions such as 'eco-friendly', 'ethical', 'sustainable' and 'responsible' fashion are often used improperly and indistinctly. The confusion derives from the fact that the relative implementation criteria overlap within the value chain, although some differences do exist.

Figure 3.1 **The taxonomy of responsible fashion.**

A simple chart can help us to visualise the relationship between eco-friendly, ethical, sustainable and responsible fashion (Fig. 3.1). With *responsible fashion* we mean a series of actions that take into consideration a broad group of stakeholders (Fig. 2.6), not solely related to the environment and society, but also other contexts such as art and culture, mass media and ethics. Returning to the 3P model—Profit, People and Planet—*sustainable fashion* aims to protect one's relationship with the environment and society by means of *eco-sustainable fashion* and *ethical fashion* respectively (see Chapter 4).

In this chapter we explore the main criteria for eco-sustainable fashion using the accounts of experts and professionals, in particular Claudia Reder (materials researcher at Material ConneXion Italia, an international library and showroom of innovative and sustainable materials) and Giusy Bettoni (founder of CLASS, a showroom with international partnerships entirely dedicated to sustainable fashion).

How can fashion companies carry out their activities in a responsible manner when choosing fabrics? Claudia Reder says: 'Responsibility in the choice of fabrics consists of controlling the value chain, using

(when possible) local products and being in direct contact with manufacturers to certify the traceability of the production process to the
end-consumer.' In fact, there are various criteria for eco-sustainability
in fashion: the main ones are described below.

- *Use of natural organic fibres and recycled or renewable syn-
  thetic resources.* In particular:
  - Natural organic fibres, for example cotton (see Section 3.1.1)
  - Biodegradable natural vegetable fibres from renewable
    sources such as flax, hemp, jute, nettle and ramie
  - Recycled natural vegetable fibres
  - Natural biodegradable fibres of animal origin such as wool,
    silk and wild silk (tussah silk), cashmere fur, mohair wool,
    angora, camel and alpaca
  - Sustainable fibres of animal origin such as recycled wool,
    organic wool and silk

Advantages and disadvantages of hemp

Hemp offers many advantages: it is easily renewable, it has a high yield,
it is an annual plant, it grows more than 3 m high and 20–30% comprised of fibrous bundles, it grows even in cold climates and has a low
environmental impact (it improves soil structure, suppresses weeds
and is resistant to pests).

It also has some disadvantages pertaining to the fibre extraction processes: maceration generates high water consumption with subsequent
pollution, and natural maceration (dew retting) needs time and suitable
weather conditions. The final option is chemical and mechanical maceration (the Setralit® process), which transforms the fibre through ultra-
sound treatment. Not all countries allow the cultivation of hemp.

Source: Material ConneXion.

- Artificial biodegradable fibres from renewable resources, some of which often have the disadvantage of being obtained from intensive crops (especially corn and soy)
- Fibres from renewable resources, such as Ingeo® (obtained from polylactic acid) and Milkofil® (obtained from casein)
- Cellulose-based fibres, which have the advantage of a production process with low environmental impact (an almost closed productive cycle) and easy biodegradability (in about

The advantages of vegetable dyeing

The main advantages of vegetable dyeing are aesthetic and environmental: natural colours are polychrome and vibrate more according to how light reflects, and they are deeper, more changeable and more iridescent than synthetic colours. The second advantage is eco-compatibility, meaning compatibility (of processing waste and of the actual coloured fabric) with the surrounding environment. Vegetable colours can allow the historical background of a particular territory to be recovered, have an economic effect on agriculture, and trigger a virtuous cycle that involves an entire value chain by conferring lifeblood to new university research and creating space for new specialised companies and new entrepreneurship. All of these reasons led Dondup, a company whose jeanswear is entirely made in Italy (and mostly made in the Marche region), to launch its Essentia jeans line in 2008 with natural dyes (guado) and natural finishing techniques.

Even so, the following factors still constrain the development of this dyeing technique: the poor ecological education of consumers and companies; the 'slowness' of the agricultural world and the lack of raw materials; costs that still remain high (as production has not yet scaled); persistent application difficulties; and solidity (i.e. stability) of the colour on the fabrics.

Source: Interview with Alessandro Butta of Cooperativa La Campana, Montefiore dell'Aso (Ascoli Piceno).

eight days), but the disadvantage of being difficult to dye. Examples are Tencel®, Lyocell, modal and bamboo/bamboo viscose, of which little is known about the chemicals used during the transformation processes)

- Synthetic fibres such as recycled polyester
- Certified dyeing and finishing processes with a low environmental impact (printing, treatments and finishing)

- *Diversification* to reduce reliance on fibres such as cotton, which is intensively cultivated, and polyester, which constitute about 80% of the textile market (Fletcher 2008; Anson and Simpson 2006)

- *Reduction, re-use and recycling of the resources* (raw materials, energy and water) necessary in all stages of the product's life-cycle, from production to consumption

- *Reduction of chemical substances* and the use of vegetable dyeing

- Vintage, second-hand and upcycling

Vintage, second-hand and upcycling

The word 'vintage' derives from the old French *vendenge* (which in turn derives from the Latin *vindemia*), which refers to fine wines. Initially coined to describe wines produced in the years with the best harvest, the term is now used more generally to define the qualities and values of a product produced at least 20 years ago. Vintage objects are considered to be cult items for various reasons, among which are superior quality compared with other earlier or later products, or elements of culture or costume.

A vintage accessory or garment is distinguished from generic second-hand pieces because the main characteristic is not that of having been used in the past, but rather the value that it has acquired progressively over time for its uniqueness and the fact that it cannot be reproduced

→

to the same high standard in modern times. It might also testify to the splendour of a bygone period or display some iconic features of a certain moment in the history of fashion, costumes or design, involving and influencing contemporary lifestyles.

Upcycling, finally, is the process of converting waste materials or useless products into better quality new materials or products with a lower environmental impact:

Source: www.clubdelmarketingedellacomunicazione.com.

Product and process certification (see Chapter 7) provides a guarantee where regulations do not impose or regulate compliance with the above criteria. Below is a list of the principal certifications in the eco-sustainable textile industry:

- *Oeko-Tex® Standard 100*. Ensures that textile products and their accessories do not contain or release substances that are harmful to human health.

- *Oeko-Tex® Standard 1000*. Adds social criteria relative, for example, to work conditions.

- *Standard 1000*. Defines the requirements a company must comply with in order to obtain ecological certification for its own production site or product.

- *Certification according to ISO 14001 and EMAS (European Eco-Management and Audit Scheme) registration*. These are a prerequisite that facilitates the achievement of the Oeko-Tex® Standard 1000®.

- *Ecolabel*. The eco-label for a European Union product. It is voluntary and applies to products made using processes with low environmental impact. It is issued on the basis of product tests and assessment of critical parameters for the production processes involved.

- *Bluesign® Standard*. Certifies not only the finished product, but forms part of a comprehensive analysis of all the components that affect production (raw materials, water, energy sources and chemical substances).

- *GOTS (Global Organic Textile Standard)*. In Italy, the ICEA (Italian Institute for Ethical and Environmental Certification) and CCPB (Consortium for the Control of Organic Products) certify products according to GOTS. GOTS-certified cotton must have at least 95% of raw materials from organic crops and meet the Basic Standards of IFOAM (International Federation of Organic Agriculture Movements).

The eco-sustainable fashion segment has generally shown clear signs of development worldwide over the last decade:

- The worldwide production of organic cotton has increased from 6,480 tonnes in 2000/01 (Ton 2002) to 242,000 tonnes in 2009/10 (Textile Exchange 2014).

- Sales of organic cotton amounted to $245 million in 2001 and have reached more than $8 billion in 2012 (Textile Exchange 2013).

- The number of certified textile companies complying with GOTS has increased steadily and significantly worldwide, from 878 in 2007 to 3,085 in 2013 (Global Standard GmbH 2014).

- In the last decade, numerous fairs and specialist exhibitions have been set up across Europe (see Table 1.1).

3.1.1 Organic cotton[1]

Cotton is cultivated in over 80 countries, with over 33 million hectares representing 2–2.5% of all cultivated land. It is one of the most

1   By Paolo Foglia, ICEA.

widespread crops in the world after wheat (200 million hectares), rice and maize (150 million hectares each) and soy (90 million hectares), and guarantees an income to over 100 million farmers and 250 million workers in the T&A sector.

The cultivation of cotton constitutes around 80% of global production of natural fibres and makes extensive use of synthetic chemical pesticides, fertilisers, growth stimulants and defoliants, which are the direct cause of reduced soil fertility, salination, loss of biodiversity, water pollution and resistance phenomena in pathogens. In order to have a more accurate grasp of this environmental impact at a global level, we need to consider that 15.7% of all insecticides and 6.8% of all pesticides are used on cotton—which, as we have said, occupies about 2.5% of the world's agricultural surface.

In the last ten years, the cultivation of cotton has been greatly affected by the spread of genetic engineering. Genetically modified cotton was first marketed in the United States in 1996 and, by 2011–12, had reached 23.8 million hectares, equivalent to 66% of the world's area dedicated to cotton.[2] Moving on to the subsequent phases of industrial processing, the main concern is represented by the water used to remove impurities, to apply colours and finishing agents, and to generate steam which is then discharged with the chemicals in it. Even here, in order to appreciate the extent of the problem we must consider that the amount of chemical and auxiliary agents added at finishing plants can be more than 1 kg per kg of processed textile product (European Commission *et al.* 2002). What emerges from this, in addition to a high risk for the environment and for the health of textile workers, is a health risk for consumers, such as the spread of allergic contact dermatitis.

Moreover, textile production has increasingly moved towards developing countries in pursuit of lower costs which are often associated with lower social and environmental guarantees.

---

2   GMO Compass, www.gmo-compass.org/eng/agri_biotechnology/gmo_planting/343.genetically_modified_cotton_global_area_under_cultivation.html.

Figure 3.2 **The drainage of Lake Aral due to cotton cultivation.**

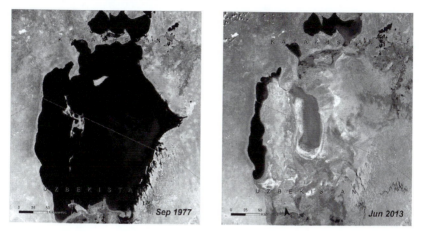

Source: UNEP, http://na.unep.net/atlas/webatlas.php?id=11.

There are several reasons to prefer organic over 'traditional' cotton. Among the most important are:

- The production of conventional cotton causes numerous deaths and diseases due to poisoning from chemical additives and pesticides. A study by the World Health Organisation (WHO and UNEP 1990) estimates that each year around 3 million people in the world are affected by forms of poisoning with severe symptoms; there are around 20,000 unintentional fatal accidents and the same amount of suicides by poisoning, and there are 735,000 cases of chronic diseases. Around a third of these accidents occur in areas of cotton cultivation.

- The conventional production of cotton has caused the drainage of 'white gold' (Fig. 3.2). In the Karakalpakstan region of Uzbekistan, the fisheries' sector used to generated over 50% of income; today, most of the population lives in poverty (Environmental Justice Foundation 2005).

Despite these valid reasons for recommending the cultivation of more sustainable raw materials, organic cotton represents today a very small share of the total, barely 1%.

3.2 From vicious circle to virtuous circle

With the data on organic cotton production as a benchmark, it is easy to estimate that the eco-sustainable fashion segment still forms an insignificant part of the total purchases in the sector. In this section we describe the elements needed for this segment to grow from a 'vicious circle' to a 'virtuous circle' as a result of collaboration by all stakeholders: consumers, institutions, companies and buyers.

3.2.1 The vicious circle

As we have seen in Section 1.2, the consumer is increasingly interested in scrutinising—and having detailed information about—the entire production chain. However, it is equally true that it is not often possible to find out everything about a product's history, origin and

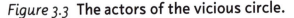

Figure 3.3 **The actors of the vicious circle.**

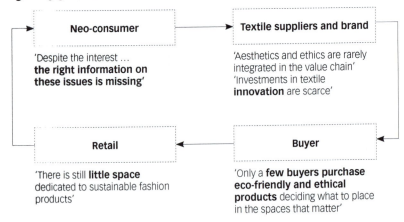

manufacturing techniques. In the vicious circle, without a clearly developed demand, companies in the T&A sector choose not to invest in innovation; buyers, in turn, do not attend fairs dedicated to sustainable fashion and shops do not devote space to these products (Fig. 3.3).

3.2.2 The virtuous circle

In order to move from a vicious circle to a virtuous circle, which is based on the creation of shared value for stakeholders, a different combination of elements is necessary:

- The continuous interest of the consumer to be informed correctly and thoroughly

- Partnerships between the various operators (buyers, companies, public institutions and mass media)

- The incorporation of aesthetics and ethics into the value chain, i.e. fashion that is first 'beautiful' and then 'good' and for which sustainability and low environmental impact are an added value justifying a *premium price*

- A culture of innovation

Figure 3.4 **The actors of the virtuous circle.**

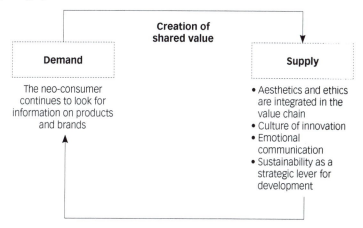

- Consumer education through dynamic and inclusive communication (see Chapter 5).

It is useful to reconsider the meaning of sustainability: not as something secondary but a strategic lever for the company, an integral part of its basic strategic orientation. This is why investments in sustainability should focus on the core business and not on the marginal business (Fig. 3.4).

3.3 Actions to reduce environmental impact along the value chain

As indicated in *Fashioning Sustainability* (Draper *et al.* 2007), T&A is 'locked into a cycle of unsustainability', in which 'the relationship between productivity (added value) and resource use has entered into a chronic and unsustainable pattern'. Figure 3.5 illustrates the

Figure 3.5 **Environmental impact for each stage of a garment's life-cycle.**

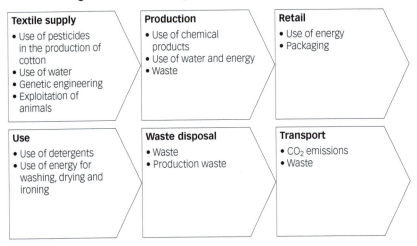

Source: Adapted from Draper *et al.* (2007).

environmental impact of a garment for each stage of the product's life-cycle.

Environmental impact is a significant part of the global impact. The 'sustainability crisis' of T&A has been exacerbated by factors such as competition from Asia, which has drastically reduced costs and quality standards, and fuelled the phenomenon of fast fashion and the demand for 'disposable' clothing. A critical element is therefore the complex and murky global supply chain, considering that production has been fragmented and the various phases transferred to different countries. The prevalence in the sector of an outsourcing logic encourages the production partners of the most important brands to use raw materials from remote areas and then subcontract to other specialised companies scattered all over the world. All this requires products to be moved from countries with low labour costs to the outlet markets with a consequent environmental impact coming from a complex logistics and transport system. The sustainability of T&A can only be improved through proactive management by the different actors involved in the sector's complex and widespread value chain.

What follows are some examples of the various critical issues faced by T&A companies along the value chain.

3.3.1 Textile supply

All types of fabric have an impact on sustainability. We have seen, for instance, how the increasing demand for cotton in the world encourages large-scale production that involves considerable use of pesticides, water and genetic engineering. Draper *et al.* (2007) point out that up to 10 tonnes of water are needed to produce a pair of jeans: inefficient use of water can cause irreversible environmental changes (like the drainage of Lake Aral). If, on the one hand, synthetic fabrics tend to be more resistant (and durable), and their production requires less energy and natural resources, on the other hand their non-renewable characteristics and low biodegradability create problems connected with their disposal.

Figure 3.6 A benchmark for sustainable raw materials.

MADE-BY ENVIRONMENTAL BENCHMARK FOR FIBRES

www.made-by.org

CLASS A	CLASS B	CLASS C	CLASS D	CLASS E	UNCLASSIFIED
Mechanically Recycled Nylon	Chemically Recycled Nylon	Conventional Flax (Linen)	Modal® (Lenzing Viscose Product)	Bamboo Viscose	Acetate
Mechanically Recycled Polyester	Chemically Recycled Polyester	Conventional Hemp	Poly-acrylic	Conventional Cotton	Alpaca Wool
Organic Flax (Linen)	CRAiLAR® Flax	PLA	Virgin Polyester	Cuprammonium Rayon	Cashmere Wool
Organic Hemp	In Conversion Cotton	Ramie		Generic Viscose	Leather
Recycled Cotton	Monocel® (Bamboo Lyocell Product)			Rayon	Mohair Wool
Recycled Wool	Organic Cotton			Spandex (Elastane)	Natural Bamboo
	TENCEL® (Lenzing Lyocell Product)			Virgin Nylon	Organic Wool
				Wool	Silk

More Sustainable

Less Sustainable

bwe This Benchmark was made in cooperation with Brown and Wilmanns Environmental, LLC. For further information on this Benchmark see www.made-by.org/benchmarks

Source: By kind permission of Made-By (www.made-by.org).

During the supply phase of raw materials, one of the most sustainable measures, apart from reduction in water consumption, is to choose the 'best' fibres: recycled or organic cotton or flax should be preferred over conventional fabrics (Fig. 3.6).

3.3.2 Production

During the production processes, in particular the dyeing, drying and finishing phases, the intensive use of chemical products and natural resources generates a high environmental impact. Apart from the consumption of considerable quantities of water and energy, many processes create non-biodegradable waste and by-products which, without waste disposal regulations, produce a risk of drinking water pollution for local inhabitants. When making production choices, companies can decide to monitor even the most remote suppliers. Obviously monitoring is just a first step: the next is to establish true partnerships for innovation.

3.3.3 Retail

Even if the use of resources and polluting agents is not expected to be as intensive as in the production phase of the T&A industry, retail tends to use considerable energy (if high energy efficiency technologies are not used) and produce considerable waste (for example, from packaging, construction and refitting). These critical issues require commitment from all companies in favour of innovative measures for the improvement of efficiency in retail.

3.3.4 Use and disposal

Washing, drying and ironing often generate the most important consumption of energy during a garment's entire life-cycle and an increasing amount of clothing that could be re-used or recycled ends up at the rubbish tip (Draper *et al.* 2007). In addition, as much as 80%

of the carbon footprint of clothes is generated post-purchase (usage phase), contributing greatly to climate change (Allwood *et al.* 2006).

During the phase in which the product is used, a good choice could be to raise consumer awareness about washing garments at low temperatures and reducing the washing frequency, offer additional buttons to extend the life of purchased garments, or provide useful guidance on corporate websites about looking after the product. Figure 3.7 shows that the highest environmental impact in the life-cycle of a pair of Levi's 501 jeans is actually generated during this phase: it is therefore fundamental to seek to inform the consumer and raise their awareness of more responsible behaviour. By the management of waste and production rejects, moreover, businesses can undertake to recycle finished products, fabrics and rejects to create new items of clothing or accessories. It is sustainable to think about a collection programme for products discarded by consumers or services for their repair or recovery.

Figure 3.7 **Environmental impact during the usage phase of a pair of jeans.**

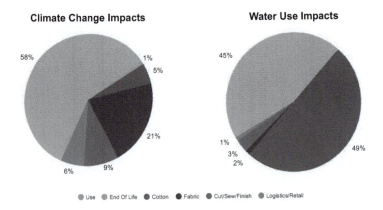

Source: http://responsiblebusiness.haas.berkeley.edu/documents/14-Haas.pdf.

3.3.5 Transport

As we have mentioned, the ever more global and complex supply chains that characterise the T&A industry involve an increased use of transport. This also includes aeroplanes due to the short production times of fast fashion, and the just-in-time flow of raw materials and finished products (air transport contributes heavily to carbon dioxide emissions). A distinction can be made between different types of transport: air transport is the most pollutant (158 kg of carbon dioxide per tonne of product), whereas sea transport is the most ecological alternative (0.7 kg of carbon dioxide per tonne of product).

Combining sea and rail transport as an alternative to air and road transport is the most sustainable choice when considering the logistics of transportation.

Even if it is not one of the most polluting sectors, T&A must become more responsible in terms of environmental sustainability. The NICE project (see Section 1.2) suggests how this can be achieved by responsible behaviour throughout the entire life-cycle of a product.

3.4 Best practice in fashion

Let's now examine some best practice in green fashion, with reference to issues which are particularly important for the various phases of the product life-cycle (Fig. 3.8):

- Innovation in the value chain
- Reduction of environmental impact and use of resources
- Greentailing
- Recycling
- Transparency and traceability of the value chain
- Green reporting

Figure 3.8 Main issues of ecological sustainability in the fashion life-cycle.

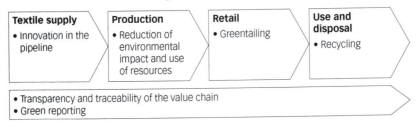

Textile supply	Production	Retail	Use and disposal
• Innovation in the pipeline	• Reduction of environmental impact and use of resources	• Greentailing	• Recycling

• Transparency and traceability of the value chain
• Green reporting

Source: Adapted from Draper *et al.* (2007).

3.4.1 Innovation in the value chain: Sinterama Newlife™[3]

For over 30 years, the Sinterama Group has been an internationally important benchmark for the production of polyester filament yarn. Having made a strategic decision to engage in responsible innovation, and with significant investment in research and development, Sinterama has brought to market Newlife™, a technological platform offering a wide range of recycled polyester threads of high quality and performance, 100% derived from post-consumption plastic bottles collected and processed entirely in Italy by mechanical and non-chemical means.

The final Newlife™ product has many applications (fashion clothing, sportswear, underwear, technical clothing, workwear, medical clothing, outdoor garments, furnishings and accident prevention textile), guaranteeing performance and quality levels which are at least equal to virgin polyester threads but with considerable savings in terms of resources and cost to the environment. Newlife™ was chosen by Armani and Valentino for Livia Firth on her first Green Carpet Challenge, and has also been used by Max Mara.

3   Source for this section: company documentation.

3.4.2 Reduction of environmental impact and use of resources: Levi's Water<Less™ jeans[4]

Eco-sustainable fashion also means reducing energy and water consumption, and not just using raw materials that have a lower impact on the environment.

An average of 45 litres of water are necessary for the washing, dyeing and finishing operations for a common pair of jeans, and a new line was produced with water savings ranging from 20 to 88%. For the autumn–winter 2011/12 collection, Levi's saved 20 million litres, equivalent to the capacity of 8.5 Olympic-sized swimming pools or water sufficient for the survival of a city of 10,000 inhabitants for over two years. Levi's achieved this ambitious goal by limiting the number of washings, by combining multiple processes in a single cycle and eliminating water from the 'stonewash' treatment.

As part of the project, Levi's also allocates 10% of the proceeds obtained from sales through the European online store to a pioneering organisation for the study and implementation of environmentally sustainable policies for water distribution in the world.

3.4.3 Greentailing: Zara's eco-sustainable store[5]

On 9 December 2010, Zara, the fast fashion colossus, opened the largest zero-impact flagship store in the world in Palazzo Bocconi in Rome, in the historic former headquarters of the La Rinascente department store. It achieved this status thanks to the following features:

- *Sustainability of the site.* The architecture was restored to Giulio De Angelis's original 1887 design which, at the time, was considered to be a ground-breaking project in its use of steel structures and very large windows.

---

4   Source for this section: http://store.levi.com/waterless/.
5   Source for this section: www.gdoweektv.it/articoli/0,1254,70_ART_3411,00.html.

- *Water use*. Installation of a recovery system which allows consumption to be reduced by over 50%.

- *Furnishings*. Made using recycled materials that are easily regenerable.

- *Air quality*. Monitoring of carbon dioxide levels, temperature and humidity to ensure greater comfort for employees and customers.

- *Energy saving*. Use of LED lamps which reduce electricity consumption by 30%, outdoor lighting which turns off when the shop is closed, and air tents which adjust to the outside temperature.

3.4.4 Recycling: Carmina Campus[6]

Carmina Campus is the brand set up at the end of 2006 by Ilaria Venturini Fendi to create bags, accessories and furniture from re-used materials. This is a sustainable creativity project responding to the current economic, environmental and social crises, in the belief that these three areas are inseparable. The philosophy of Carmina Campus to separate itself from the production circuit by only using 'second life' or discarded materials leads to collections which are not necessarily seasonal but rather share a material or a concept, as well as making the same products but with different raw materials.

The brand worked in Cameroon from 2007 to 2009 with an independent project involving a community of marginalised women. Subsequently, a project was set up in Kenya and Uganda thanks to collaboration with the ITC (International Trade Center, a joint UN and World Trade Organisation agency). In Kenya in particular there is stable production of semi-finished products for bags and a 100% 'made in Africa' line. The logic behind the African project, which can

6   Sources for this section: www.carminacampus.com and www.vogue.it/en/talents/new-talents/2010/07/carmina-campus.

be summed up in the Aid for Trade motto 'Not Charity Just Work', is to bring Carmina Campus's know-how to the southern hemisphere, offering job opportunities to marginalised people who receive training and technical assistance through the ITC in order to be able to work with professionals. The brand has also launched some special projects with other companies such as Campari and Mini (BMW group).

3.4.5 Transparency and traceability of the value chain: Patagonia and Monnalisa

Patagonia[7]

Patagonia's philosophy is summed up in its corporate mission statement: 'Build the best product, cause no unnecessary harm, use business to inspire and implement solutions for the environmental crisis.' Yvon Chouinard, founder of Patagonia, began climbing in 1953 at the age of 14. At the time, as pitons were made from steel, he realised that it was a good idea to replace them with aluminium. This had less of an impact on the rock as they were easier to extract without leaving any trace. 'Clean climbing' was born.

Having started with mountaineering, which remians Patagonia's core business, the company now covers a wide range of sports— including skiing, snowboarding, surfing and fly fishing—all of which are considered 'silent sports' as they take place without engines and guarantee a greater interaction with nature. The approach to product design shows a tendency towards simplicity and functionality: it is telling that Patagonia's iconic and bestselling product is the pile fleece jacket, first introduced in 1977.

The company's eco-sustainability can be summarised by some key initiatives:

7   Source for this section: www.patagonia.com.

- *1% for the Planet.* Patagonia donates 1% of sales to hundreds of projects which work towards reducing negative environmental impact all over the world.

- *The use of environmentally sustainable materials.* Since its early years of activity, Patagonia has invested in the research and development of fibres such as recycled polyester and organic cotton, with the overall objective of reducing the environmental impact of each stage of production.

- *The Common Threads Initiative.* This defines the series of commitments that Patagonia wants to take on—consumer awareness and involvement—to reduce environmental impact (see Section 5.3.3).

The transparency and traceability of the value chain represent a strong element of differentiation for Patagonia compared with other sportswear brands: a section of its website, 'The Footprint Chronicles',[8] provides a detailed list of all suppliers with their main information. Transparent communication of business behaviour is guaranteed by *The Cleanest Line*,[9] a blog for employees, friends and clients dealing with various topics on environmental sustainability and sustainable lifestyles in an experiential and involving manner.

Monnalisa[10]

Monnalisa, an Italian clothing company for children and one of the international market leaders in the sector, has for years been actively committed to environmental and social responsibility in order to establish the means for structured dialogue with its stakeholders. Of particular note is a product traceability project which was launched in 2011.[11]

---

8   www.patagonia.com/eu/enNL/patagonia.go?assetid=67366.
9   www.thecleanestline.com.
10 Sources for this section: http://portal.monnalisa.eu/about_the_group_en/ social_responsibility/corporate_social_responsibility.aspx   and   company documentation.
11 What follows is an extract from an interview with Sara Tommasiello, Finance and Control Manager, Human Resources, CSR Manager, Monnalisa.

The company defines traceability as a complete set of information about the origin of the product which allows its history to be reconstructed by means of the identification and documentation of all activities, materials used and companies involved in its production. This therefore means the ability to keep track of production along the supply chain, from the location in which the first processing takes place to the production of the finished product and its placement on the market. Furthermore, the traceability system gives the customer greater awareness of quality at the point of purchase, thus reinforcing the quality of the brand.

The smart labelling project is part of a wider 'integrated value chain through RFID [radio-frequency identification] technologies' project, which provides for the use of RF technology. Those principally involved in the study and development of smart labelling are managers in the areas of project operations, ICT, supply chain, retail and e-commerce. At present, around 50% of Monnalisa garments are equipped with a smart label and the end-consumer is able to look up information regarding the traceability and originality of the product in the following ways:

- By scanning the QR code printed on the back of the data label

- By going to a special section of the Monnalisa website and entering the unique identification code printed on the label (Fig. 3.9)[12]

- By placing the product near an intelligent device (iPad, screen or touch-screen table) located in shops for interaction with consumers

The project has entailed specific investment in smart labels, RFID printers and the development of an ad hoc software platform to link the RFID tag's EPC (Electronic Product Code) to the relevant product information.

---

12   http://portal.monnalisa.eu/about_the_group_en/company_profile_en-US/ traceability.aspx.

Figure 3.9 **Traceability card for a Monnalisa garment.**

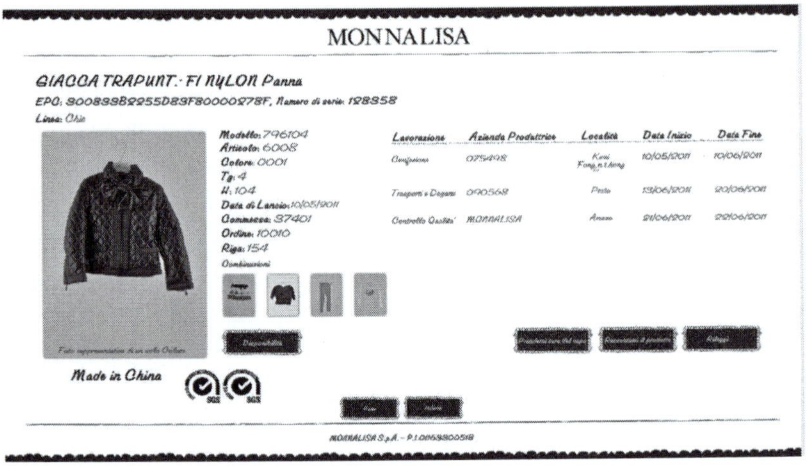

Source: www.monnalisa.eu.

3.4.6 Green reporting: Puma

In 2010, the sportswear brand Puma, part of the Kering group, launched the 'Environmental Profit&Loss' green reporting system for the analysis and economic assessment of the company's environmental impact, including business operations and the supply chain (Natural Capital Accounting). The main purpose of green reporting is to allow managers and other stakeholders to assess the extent of these impacts and where they take place along the value chain: it represents a scale to measure and monitor the impact of the operations carried out by the company and its suppliers, starting right from the initial raw materials. It is a tool to:

- Communicate the importance of the environment for the company's sustainability
- Improve transparency regarding the company's supply chain
- Improve risk management with regards to environmental impact
- Support a more holistic view of business performance by speaking to stakeholders with clarity and transparency
- Identify opportunities to improve product sustainability

3.5 Towards 'cradle-to-cradle'

The system which currently dominates industrial production is defined as 'from the cradle to the grave', a process which follows a linear and one-way model: resources are extracted, processed into a product, sold and finally eliminated, buried in a kind of 'grave', usually a rubbish tip or an incinerator. The cradle-to-cradle project and certification aims at creating a 'closed circle' which, instead of ending with disposal, considers the waste product as a nourishing factor to be reincorporated in a 'continuous closed cycle' without any energy or physical materials being wasted. In *Cradle to Cradle: Remaking the Way We Make Things* (2002), the inventor William McDonough and his colleague and chemist Michael Braungart wrote a cradle-to-cradle manifesto based on the possibility of transforming waste into goods and services which in turn generate environmental, social and economic value.

In general, the principle suggests that any decision may not be the correct one if we only consider one part of the product's life-cycle: in order to be truly environmentally friendly we must begin with an analysis that determines the environmental impact of every stage, from preproduction and production, to usage, recycling and disposal.

References and further reading

Allwood, Julian M., Søren Ellebaek Laursen, Cecilia Malvido de Rodríguez and Nancy M.P. Bocken (2006) *Well Dressed?* (Cambridge, UK: University of Cambridge Institute of Manufacturing).

Anson, Robin, and Paul Simpson (2006) 'Global Trend in Fibre Prices, Production and Consumption', *Textiles Outlook International* 125: 82-106.

Draper, Stephanie, Vicky Murray and Ilka Weissbrod (2007) *Fashioning Sustainability: A Review of the Sustainability Impacts on the Clothing Industry* (London: Forum for the Future).

Environmental Justice Foundation (2005) *White Gold: The True Cost of Cotton. Uzbekistan, Cotton and the Crushing of a Nation* (London: EJF Foundation).

European Commission (2003) *Integrated Pollution Prevention and Control. Reference Document on Best Available Techniques for the Textiles Industry* (Brussels: European Commission).

European Commission, Directorate-General Joint Research Centre (JRC), Institute for Prospective Technological Studies (Seville), Technologies for Sustainable Development European IPPC Bureau (2002) *Reference Document on Best Available Techniques for the Textiles Industry* (Brussels: European Commission).

Global Standard GmbH (2014) *GOTS Annual Report 2013*, www.global-standard.org/images/stories/Annual_Reports/AR_Public_2013_lowres.pdf.

Fletcher, Kate (2008) *Sustainable Fashion and Textiles: Design Journeys* (London: Earthscan).

Hethorn, Janet, and Connie Ulasewicz (2008) *Sustainable Fashion: Why Now? A Conversation Exploring Issues, Practices, and Possibilities* (New York: Fairchild Books).

Laursen, Søren Ellebaek, and John Hansen (eds.) (1997) *EDIPTEX: Environmental Assessment of Textiles. Working Report No. 24* (Copenhagen: Danish Environmental Protection Agency).

McDonough, William, and Michael Braungart (2002) *Cradle to Cradle: Remaking the Way We Make Things* (New York: North Point Press).

Pieraccini, Silvia (2009) 'Eco-moda: all'etica si aggiunge la bellezza', *Il Sole 24 Ore*, 18 April.

Reina, Davide, and Silvia Vianello (2011) *GreenWebEconomics. La nuova frontiera* (Milan: Egea).

Rinaldi, Francesca Romana (2011) 'Moda eco-sostenibile: opportunità e rischi', *Les Cahiers Fashion Marketing*, http://lescahiersfm.com/it/articoli/98-modaeco-sostenibile-di-francesca-rinaldi.html.

Textile Exchange (2013) *2012 Organic Cotton Market Report*, http://textileexchange.org/2012-Market-Report.

—— (2014) *2013 Organic Cotton Report. From farm to market*, http://textileexchange.org/publications/2013-organic-cotton-report.

Ton, P. (2002) *The international market for organic cotton and eco-textiles: a 2001 market survey* (London: PAN UK).

WHO and UNEP (1990) *Public Health Impact of Pesticides Used in Agriculture* (Geneva, WHO).

4
Fashion and society

by Francesca Romana Rinaldi and Stefano Pogutz[1]

> People can only live fully by helping others to live. When you give life to friends you truly live. Cultures can only realise their further richness by honouring other traditions. And only by respecting natural life, can humanity continue to exist.
>
> Daisaku Ikeda

4.1 The relationship between fashion and society

The relationship between companies and society is becoming ever more complex. Some issues are increasingly important: what are the expectations of society towards companies and the way they operate? More generally, what is the role of the company in society today? Ethical fashion is the aspect of responsible fashion that deals with the relationship binding the company and 'society' and attempts to answer the questions set forth above: so-called 'ethical' fashion is independent from the concept of business ethics, which will be examined in

---

1   Stefano Pogutz collaborated on Sections 4.2–4.5 and wrote Section 4.10.2.

Chapter 9, analysing the relationship between the fashion company and the macro-environment of business ethics. We once again refer to the *stakeholder view* (see Section 2.1) and to the subdivision of stakeholders into two categories: *primary*, associated with the core business of the company (suppliers, employees and collaborators) and *secondary* (consumers, civil society in general and minorities).

This chapter illustrates the main areas in which a responsible company can act to improve its relationship with society while taking into account the legislative framework (see Chapter 7).

The company's social dimension develops in a variety of ways:

- *Labour and human rights.* This concerns all aspects relating to the practices of the company towards employees and the protection of human rights (for example, freedom of association and equal opportunities).

- *Governance, anti-corruption and fair practices.* This includes all aspects of the organisation and governance of the company, including market practices (for example, fair competition).

- *Society and community development.* This refers to the impact of the organisation on social systems and the environmental conditions of the communities in which it operates.

- *Product and consumer-related responsibility.* This concerns all of the organisation's products and services and includes issues such as health and safety of customers/consumers, information and labelling, marketing and privacy.

- *Relationship with suppliers.* This concerns every aspect of the relationship between the firm and its suppliers along the value chain (for example, compliance with payment deadlines, or the enforcement of codes of conduct).

The subject of labour has a particularly crucial role in the relationship between fashion and society. In this context the ILO[2] fulfils a very important function. In fact, a large part of CSR initiatives, including codes of conduct, refer to principles based on international standards regulating labour.

As already noted, over the last few decades fashion businesses have increasingly outsourced their production to subcontractors located in emerging countries like India, China, Pakistan, Indonesia, Vietnam and many Latin American regions. The search for low-cost labour and proximity to sources of raw materials have favoured the rapid transformation of supply chains. As a result of this dynamic, firms have endured increasing pressure from governments, consumers and NGOs to extend CSR practices to their production lines, including not only first-tier suppliers but second- and third-tier ones as well. This task is very demanding because the implementation of CSR programmes (for example, the adoption of codes of conduct) and the monitoring of suppliers at a global level require specific professional skills and considerable financial resources. In the following sections, we shall examine strategies for social responsibility in the workplace and briefly analyse the fundamental rights of workers:

- Freedom of association and collective bargaining

- Abolition of forced labour and child labour

- Elimination of all forms of discrimination in the workplace

These categories of rights are addressed by the Declaration of Fundamental Principles and Rights at Work adopted in 1998 by the ILO. This 'fundamental declaration' expresses the commitment by governments, employers and workers' organisations to acknowledge that the principles and rights mentioned above are universal because they constitute a prerequisite for social justice. These standards are commonly

2   In 2009, the ILO set up a help-desk for firms aimed at providing guidance in applying the principles included in international labour standards (www.ilo.org/empent/areas/business-helpdesk/lang--en/index.htm).

cited in almost all initiatives in the CSR field: complying with them and contributing towards their promotion are essential conditions for a company that wants to be socially responsible.

The second fundamental pillar that contributes towards defining the relationship between business, human rights and rights at work is the document *Guiding Principles on Business and Human Rights*, which is discussed in the next section.

4.2 The United Nations *Protect, Respect and Remedy* framework

In June 2011, the UN Human Rights Council adopted the *Guiding Principles on Business and Human Rights: Implementing the United Nations 'Protect, Respect and Remedy' Framework*. The result of lengthy research and consultation which started in 2005 under the guidance of John G. Ruggie, the dossier offers an innovative approach to dealing with the growing impact of multinational companies and transnational economic activities on the issue of human rights. The *Protect, Respect and Remedy* framework is based on three principles:

- *Protect*. Nation states have a duty to protect human rights from violations by third parties, including companies, through policies and appropriate judicial standards and procedures.

- *Respect*. Companies are responsible for respecting human rights, acting with due diligence to avoid violation, and for dealing with any negative impacts which may arise.

- *Remedy*. Nation states and companies are responsible for improving access to effective appeal, be it judicial or non-judicial, for victims of abuse.

The framework does not establish new legal obligations for companies or states, but provides an innovative approach to protecting a series of fundamental rights and principles.

From public scandals to social responsibility: Nike

Nike, the largest retailer of sports products in the world, produces and distributes footwear, clothing, equipment and accessories for sports and leisure. The company operates in more than 160 countries with around 700 supply factories. Conditions for suppliers and subcontractors have always been the cause for heated debate regarding poor working conditions, harassment and abuse of fundamental workers' rights. During the second half of the 1990s, Nike was accused of using child labour in developing countries and of exploiting its workers. In 1998, even the founder and CEO Phil Knight had to acknowledge that Nike products were synonymous with very low wages and forced overtime labour.

The Nike experience shows how the general public, media and NGOs can use reputation and brand image as a lever to put pressure on firms, thereby inducing rapid changes in a company's behaviour and strategy.

After the scandals of the late 1990s, Nike responded to its critics by developing measures such as codes of conduct, by auditing compliance with control procedures, by increasing wages and by introducing policies for the compensation of workers. This approach has helped the biggest sports shoes brand in the world to rebuild its image at a global level, to the extent that it is now recognised as a trailblazer for CSR standards in the clothing sector.

Audit

Nike has implemented various audit tools to promote transparency. In particular, the company has developed three types of audit:

- *MAV (Management Audit Verification).* A tool to analyse the causes and impacts of non-compliance by focusing on the issues of working hours, wages and freedom of association, and the development of complaint systems followed by the verification of action plans to remedy non-compliance with both local laws and the Nike code of conduct.

→

- *SHAPE (Safety Health Attitude of Management People and Environment)*. An audit tool used by a factory to determine compliance with Nike code standards.

- *ESH (Environmental Safety and Health)*. A comprehensive audit tool used to determine compliance with Nike code standards.

Code of conduct

Nike has also developed and implemented a code of conduct to clarify and raise expectations for suppliers, and to define the minimum standard that each factory must satisfy. Nike was one of the first companies to support the UN Global Compact[3] when it was launched in 2000, as a strategic policy initiative for companies engaged in aligning their operations and strategies with ten principles in the area of human rights, labour, environment and anti-corruption.

Source: http://nikeinc.com/system/assets/2806/Nike_Code_of_Conduct_original.pdf ?1317156854.

3   'The Global Compact asks companies to embrace universal principles and to partner with the United Nations. It has grown to become a critical platform for the UN to engage effectively with enlightened global business' (Ban Ki-moon, UN General Secretary, www.unglobalcompact.org). The ten Global Compact principles concern human rights (1–2), labour (3–6), environment (7–9) and corruption (10). Principle 1: Companies should support and respect the protection of internationally proclaimed human rights and, Principle 2: make sure that they are not complicit in human rights abuses. Principle 3: Companies should uphold freedom of association and the effective recognition of the right to collective bargaining. Principle 4: They should collaborate towards the elimination of all forms of forced and compulsory labour. Principle 5: They should support the effective abolition of child labour. Principle 6: They should work towards the elimination of discrimination at work. Principle 7: Companies should support a preventive approach to environmental challenges. Principle 8: They should undertake initiatives to promote greater environmental responsibility. Principle 9: They should encourage the development and diffusion of environmentally friendly technologies. Principle 10: Companies should work against corruption in all its forms, including extortion and bribery. See also Section 7.3.2.

4.3 Freedom of association and collective bargaining

Social dialogue and freedom of association are two important elements of CSR policy when referring to labour and human rights issues.

Social dialogue identifies all types of negotiations, consultations or exchange of information between the representatives of governments, employers and workers on matters of shared concern pertaining to economic and social policy. Freedom of association is a fundamental human right and is one of the fundamental principles underlying social dialogue.

Freedom of association is defined as the individual right to meet other individuals and collectively express, promote, pursue and defend common interests. With regards to the workplace, it means the right of workers and employees to organise themselves freely and voluntarily.

Levi Strauss & Co.

Founded in 1853, Levi Strauss & Co. (LS&Co) is a multinational American company operating in the clothing sector (in particular jeans and trousers), with a turnover of $4.7 billion and over 17,000 employees (2013). The company first adopted a code of conduct for its suppliers in 1991, based on the ILO core conventions, the main international conventions for the protection of human rights.

Over the years, LS&Co has implemented a comprehensive programme to evaluate non-compliance with the standards and to identify procedures for improvement should problems arise. In fact, LS&Co considers the monitoring of suppliers as just one part of a wider process of improving working conditions, and has directly initiated programmes to protect and strengthen the rights of workers in various communities. In addition, the company collaborates with the governments of various emerging countries in order to consolidate laws protecting workers and to promote their effective implementation.

→

The facts

In 1991, LS&Co was the first multinational company in the field of cloth-ing and fashion to define and implement a broad and well-developed code of conduct for its suppliers, aimed at protecting workers' rights. LS&Co established the following:

> LS&Co declared to respect the right of workers to constitute indepen-dent organisations or to choose which organisation to join, respect-ing their right to collective bargaining. LS&Co expeced their suppliers to comply with the law on freedom of association and on collective bargaining. Their business partners should ensure that workers who decide to participate in these organisations were not subject to any form of discrimination or disciplinary or punitive actions, and that the representatives of these organisations could contact and involve their associates according to the conditions governed by law or by agree-ments between the workers and their unions.[4]

Despite the existence of this mechanism, some international organi-sations reported to LS&Co in March 2004 that 31 workers, employed by a supplier in Ouanaminthe (Haiti), had been dismissed as a result of trying to form a trade union association. After having ascertained the facts, LS&Co had the workers reinstated in April 2004. However, despite the reinstatement and the American company's action, vari-ous NGOs continued to report violations of workers' rights, while the supplier stated that the workers had infringed company rules. In this period, the supplier's productivity dropped significantly to the extent that LS&Co's deadlines were not met and the level of orders had to be modified.

LS&Co decided to maintain the contractual relationship, but under specific conditions: the company would have to enforce the 'Terms of Engagement' and respect rights such as freedom of association and collective bargaining. In February 2005, the company management and the new trade union reached an initial agreement and in December

---

4   http://lsco.s3.amazonaws.com/wp-content/uploads/2014/01/Case-Study_ Freedom-of-Association-A-Positive-Resutl-in-Haiti.pdf.

→

2005 the first collective bargaining was completed. The freely negotiated agreement was enforced in January 2006.

Source: Adapted from www.levistrauss.com/sustainability/innovative-practices/people/worker-rights/ and http://lsco.s3.amazonaws.com/wp-content/uploads/2014/01/LSCO-Sustainability-Guidebook-2013-_-December.pdf.

4.4 Forced labour and child labour

The abolition of child labour and forced labour sets out two fundamental rights promoted by the ILO and represents a basic principle for the implementation of every CSR policy.

ILO Convention no. 29 (1930) defines forced labour as every job or service obtained under the threat of punishment and which the person did not volunteer to carry out. Forced labour continues to exist in most developing countries. According to ILO estimates,[5] the issue involves at least 12.3 million individuals throughout the world.

Child labour, and any type of employment or labour that by its nature or the circumstances in which it takes place is detrimental to the intellectual, physical, social and moral development of young people, undermines their education by preventing them from attending school, forcing them to drop out early or obliging them to work and study at the same time. From the point of view of labour rights, two fundamental conventions govern the issue:

- ILO Convention no. 138 (1973) on the minimum working age
- ILO Convention no. 182 (1999) on the worst forms of child labour

5   http://ilo.org/global/standards/subjects-covered-by-international-labour-standards/forced-labour/lang--en/index.htm.

The two conventions identify as 'children' those under 18 years of age, and the following two categories as 'child labour' to be abolished:[6]

- Work carried out by a child under the minimum age (14, 15 or 16 years) recognised for a certain type of work (as defined by national legislation in accordance with international rules) such that it compromises the education and full development of the child

- The worst forms of child labour (such as slavery, child trafficking, imprisonment for debt, forced labour, forced recruitment of children for their use in armed conflicts, child prostitution and pornography and all illegal activities), and work that, for its nature or the circumstances in which it is carried out, can affect the health, safety and morality of the minor.

In 2010, according to UN data,[7] 215 million children (under 18 years of age) were doing what is considered to be child labour every day. Of these, over 115 million were carrying out particularly hazardous jobs, including the worst forms of labour mentioned in the second point above.

Responsible Cotton Network and the fight against forced child labour in Uzbekistan

The Responsible Cotton Network is a network of brands, retail associations, investors and civil society working collaboratively to halt the use of forced child labour in Uzbek cotton production. Founded in May 2008, the network works with both US and European companies to combat forced child labour in their supply chains.

---

6   http://ilo.org/global/standards/subjects-covered-by-international-labour-standards/child-labour/lang--en/index.htm.

7   www.un.org/en/events/childlabourday/background.shtml.

→

Problem: allegations of forced child labour cause serious concern among investors

An estimated 2 million children between the ages of 11 and 17 harvest cotton in Uzbekistan under conditions described as forced labour. Unlike where children work on family farms, the Uzbek case is distinguished by its scale, organisation and government complicity. Each year, for example, the government closes schools, hospitals and offices for three months in order to use students, teachers and government employees to boost the workforce available for the annual cotton harvest. The Responsible Cotton Network says some school administrators have used physical abuse and public humiliation to ensure that the government-imposed quota of 30–60 kg of cotton per child per day, depending on age, is picked. The Network also notes that these children receive little or no pay for their work, and are often only provided with food.

Solution

In 2005, NGOs (including the Environmental Justice Foundation and the International Crisis Group), Uzbek advocacy groups and the British Broadcasting Corporation, began to raise awareness about the issue and mounted a strong campaign for companies to remove Uzbek cotton from their supply chains.

After a successful campaign, this NGO coalition began to work with investors and companies in what would later become known as the Responsible Cotton Network. As a result, many clothing companies came under heavy pressure to exclude Uzbek cotton from their supply chains, in order to ensure they were not complicit in the violation of these children's rights. Nonetheless, when companies were confronted by the problem, many insisted that traceability within the chain was too complex and they could not determine whether or not Uzbek cotton was used in their product lines. In particular, they noted the challenge posed by the fact that Uzbek cotton is sold on commodity exchanges and then traded and mixed with cotton from other countries.

Since its foundation, the Responsible Cotton Network has given new impetus to the fight against child labour by convening meetings and

→

webinars, collating information, and seeking to influence policymakers in Uzbekistan through diplomatic channels.

Results

One of the positive outcomes of this dilemma is the considerable progress made by companies with regards to the traceability of cotton. In fact, suppliers are now asked to demonstrate provenance and show certificates of origin for the raw material. Moreover, a wide range of companies have also publicly announced that they will not knowingly source cotton from Uzbekistan, including: American Eagle Outfitters, C&A, GAP, Levi Strauss & Co., Macy's, Nike, North Face, Patagonia, Tesco, Timberland, Vanity Fair Corporation and Walmart.

Source: Adapted from http://human-rights.unglobalcompact.org/case_studies/forced-labour/forced_labour/combating_forced_child_labour_in_uzbekistan.html.

4.5 Discrimination in the workplace

Issues related to diversity and equality or, more generally, to discrimination in the workplace, are becoming increasingly important for businesses all over the world. One of the most important and complex challenges is to ensure equality of gender in countries where cultural norms, laws or rules for the management of business allow and promote discrimination (for example, against women or religious minorities). In the 1958 Discrimination (Employment and Occupation) Convention, ILO defined the issue as 'any distinction, exclusion or preference made on the basis of race, colour, sex, religion, political opinion, national extraction or social origin, which has the effect of nullifying or impairing equality of opportunity or treatment in employment or occupation'. In recent years, many firms have created initiatives to promote the value of diversity in enhancing their activities and improving working conditions and business results.

Dealing with cases of abuse against women: the Timberland experience

Timberland is an international brand operating in the footwear, sportswear and accessories sector. In 2012, turnover was around $1.7 billion and it employed more than 6,000 people. The company manages its own shops but also sells through independent multi-brand shops, department stores and e-commerce. Timberland has over 460 suppliers located all over the world, for which it enforces its own code of conduct and auditing and rating methodologies. Over the years, it has developed a comprehensive CSR policy and implemented several programmes and activities to protect the environment and the communities in which it operates.

Problem: human rights violations and lack of life skills[8] among female workers in Bangladesh

Timberland has a significant supplier workforce in Bangladesh. For example, one of the company's key suppliers, YoungOne, has an 85% female workforce. Timberland's international NGO partner, CARE, has conducted research in the country, showing that women face domestic violence, harassment, rape and torture. CARE also found that many women were unaware of their human rights in these and other respects.

Solution

Timberland has launched a programme—carried out through CARE and its local NGO partner MAMATA—to raise awareness among women

---

8   The term 'life skill' generally refers to a range of basic cognitive, emotional and relational abilities enabling a person to operate with competence at both an individual and a social level. They are abilities and skills which enable a person to learn versatile and positive behaviour thanks to which it is possible to deal effectively with the requests and challenges of daily life. The fundamental core life skills identified by the World Health Organisation comprise ten competences which can be grouped into three categories: emotional (self-awareness, managing emotions, stress management), cognitive (problem-solving, decision-making, critical sense, creativity) and social (empathy, effective communication, effective relationships).

→

about their rights and to provide social infrastructure among 24,000 employees at YoungOne factories in the Chittagong Export Processing Zone. The programme helps to create a support network of workers, law enforcement officers and other organisations to protect the rights of workers, 85% of whom are migrant women from rural areas in Bangladesh. Timberland has invested more than $480,000 in the programme over seven years and has also financed a medical fund to assist low-income workers. CARE replenishes medicines and provides staffing for the clinic. CARE has also created a micro-finance facility for YoungOne employees, granting access to small loans for education, healthcare and business initiatives. One of the goals of the programme is to become independent of Timberland and CARE, so that MAMATA can run the programme directly.

Results

The results can be summarised as increased awareness of rights, of healthcare and of access to credit. In 2008, 4,739 workers received training on the topics of labour law, health, hygiene, HIV/AIDS, gender rights, abuse and human trafficking.

Through access to micro-credit, employees and their relatives have been able to open small businesses such as barber shops, clothing repair shops and refreshment stands. By the end of 2008, the programme had reached 17,500 people and provided more than $2.6 million in loans. Also in 2008 the medical clinic treated around 560 patients.

According to a recent report from Timberland, 'Timberland and CARE are eager to apply this model of success to facilitate the creation of Sustainable Living Environments in other regions of need.'

Source: Adapted from http://human-rights.unglobalcompact.org/case_studies/gender/gender/addressing_wider_abuses_against_women.html.

4.6 Work–life balance

As we have seen by analysing the topic of social responsibility in the fashion industry, workers are one of the key stakeholders. One aspect that has become increasingly important in recent years is that of ensuring employees have the necessary conditions for a healthy and balanced life inside and outside the company. Complying with contractual working hours is a start: particularly during periods of crisis or recession, the worker experiences increasingly excessive hours which are barely sustainable in terms of the person's psycho-physical balance, and particularly for their work–life balance. The provision

Figure 4.1 **Corporate nursery school and canteen at the Tod's headquarters in the Marche region.**

Photos by Francesca Romana Rinaldi.

Figure 4.2 **The 'Della Valle' primary school in Casette d'Ete.**

Source: Company brochure (courtesy of Tod's).

within the company of comfortable environments and facilities for workers is one aspect of this responsibility, with nurseries, gyms and canteens being the most widespread examples.

The Tod's group, a leading producer of Italian luxury shoes, has for some years been offering its employees the opportunity for their children to attend the company nursery (Fig. 4.1). At the company headquarters in Sant'Elpidio a Mare in the Marche region, employees can have lunch in the canteen or spend their free time in the gym. Tod's has also financed the construction of the 'Della Valle' primary school in Casette d'Ete, a hamlet near to Sant'Elpidio a Mare (Fig. 4.2).

4.7 Corporate philanthropy

The relationship between fashion and society can be analysed from many points of view: as already mentioned, there are several different stakeholders that fall under the main category 'society' (not only consumers, employees, collaborators and suppliers, but also citizens, minorities, etc.).

In general, philanthropic philosophies mean funding for nonprofit activities, the so-called 'grant making' which is often a key part of funding socio-cultural activities. In other instances, programmes and projects are taken up directly by the company, operating through appropriate divisions.

Foundations are endowed when companies decide to outsource their philanthropic deeds. The primary task of corporate foundations is the social redistribution of part of the economic value produced by the company, which is then used to fund and promote charity initiatives. As discrete entities, such foundations represent and promote an autonomous and often strategic concept of the firm's philanthropy, of which the foundation itself is the most common expression.

One specific form of corporate philanthropy consists of the working hours that employees dedicate to volunteer activities: Timberland's 'Path of Service' programme belongs to this category.

Timberland 'Path of Service' 2012: 20 years of social work

Since 1992, the then new and innovative 'Path of Service' programme created by former CEO Jeff Swartz and now supported and encouraged by VF Corporation, has enabled every Timberland employee to dedicate 40 hours per year to community service at a local level, and has led to the organisation of various annual events at a global level, including 'Earth Day' in April and 'Serv-a-Palooza' in October. With the direct involvement of nonprofit associations, 'Path of Service' has enabled urban/environmental conservation and reclamation projects to take place in disused areas or those affected by natural disasters where ecological and social intervention has been required. A total of 844,955 hours of volunteer work have been donated since 1992, in over 30 countries in which the brand is present and involving over 79% of the workforce.

Source: Company documentation.

The Stella McCartney brand is perceived as especially sustainable given the lifestyle and personality of the eponymous fashion designer, a vegan and rights activist. In addition to banning leather from its collections, the brand's philanthropic initiatives include support for PETA (People for the Ethical Treatment of Animals) and organising 'Meat Free Monday', a consumer awareness programme about the consequences of environmental change resulting from the production and consumption of meat.

Another example is Tod's, which has set up several philanthropic initiatives including the restoration of the Colosseum: in July 2011, after a heated debate about whether to allow a company to pay for public works in exchange for advertising rights, funding of €25 million was approved to restore the monument after damage caused by earthquakes, smog and daily traffic. Thanks to this funding the Colosseum, and its almost two millennia of history, will from 2015 continue to welcome millions of tourists every year.

4.8 Fashion and fair trade

Talking about the balance between a fashion company and society means first talking about fair trade. Fair trade is part of the broader concept of social and environmental responsibility and focuses on the initial phases of the supply chain, in particular the needs of small farmers/producers and core issues such as a fair price, decent working conditions, support for the local community and fair commercial terms for farmers and workers in emerging and developing economies. Fair trade sets out ten principles established by the WFTO (World Fair Trade Organisation):[9]

- Creating opportunities for economically disadvantaged producers
- Transparency and accountability
- Social, economic and environmental fair trading practices
- Payment of a fair price to producers
- Ensuring no child labour or forced labour
- Commitment to non-discrimination, gender equity and freedom of association
- Ensuring good working conditions
- Providing capacity building for producers
- Promotion of fair trade
- Respect for the environment

Many companies in the fashion sector have decided to go down the path of fair trade in recent years: People Tree is one of the first and best-known international companies (see Section 5.3.2), while in

---

9   www.wfto.com/index.php?option=com_content&task=view&id=2 &Itemid=14. WFTO is the world organisation for fair trade. Prior to March 2009 it was called IFAT (International Federation of Alternative Trade).

Italy noteworthy initiatives are Solidal Coop designed by Katharine Hamnett[10] and the Auteurs du Monde label from CMT Altromercato, designed by Marina Spadafora.[11]

4.9 Other forms of ethical fashion: 'made in prison' and the valorisation of local production expertise

When we talk about ethical fashion, we may refer also to a type of activity that has a positive outcome for more disadvantaged stakeholders such as some minority groups (non-integrated ethnic groups, disabled people, prisoners and so on) or to the promotion of expertise and production techniques pertinent to particular areas. Examples of this second interpretation are the Malìparmi brand with its 'needle-embroidered' (*suzani* technique) handmade articles or iconic products embellished with bead embroideries typical of India and Indonesia, and Gabriella Ghidoni's 'Royah' project which trawls the cultural richness of Afghanistan to create contemporary items of clothing in the Western taste.

> Goods available on the market increasingly have a communicative and symbolic value: they are able to indicate who we are, what we want, how we live and which symbolic universe we want to be a part of. The emergence of responsible consumption offers a further confirmation of these ideas and reiterates that many different criteria guide consumers in their purchasing decisions because they are not only looking for material satisfaction, but also for sentimental and valorial gratification (Lunghi and Montagni 2007).

10   www.vestosolidal.it.
11   www.altromercato.it/auteurs-du-monde/auteurs-du-monde.

'Made in prison' fashion responds to this search for valorial gratification: by making the purchase, the consumer helps provide the prisoner with the chance of work while in prison, which improves daily life conditions and creates an opportunity for social redemption. Some of the brands which have moved towards fashion produced by prisoners are Sartoria San Vittore, I Gatti Galeotti and Made in Carcere ('carcere' is the Italian word for prison), belonging to three co-operatives operating in San Vittore (Milan), Lecce and Trani prisons. 'These are economic realities at the margins of the mainstream, struggling at times with problems of economic sustainability, a delicate balance in a highly competitive market, but combining social needs with interesting product innovations' (Lunghi 2012).

Made in Carcere

The Made in Carcere brand was founded in 2007 thanks to the inspiration and will of Luciana Delle Donne, a former top manager in the banking sector who embarked on the Officina Creativa scs (a nonprofit social co-operative) project. The brand's designers and artisans are 20 special women: inmates of Lecce and Trani prisons who are offered a second chance. 'A second chance for the reject fabrics, silk, leather and cotton which become bags and accessories, alongside social redemption, through the work of these women involved in the project,' says Luciana Delle Donne.

4.10 Best practice in fashion

4.10.1 The responsible value chain: Gucci

One of the most popular luxury brands in the world, Gucci, owned by the French group Kering, set out on a definite path of social responsibility some years ago. Rossella Ravagli, head of CSR and sustainability at Gucci, spoke to us in an interview:

> The culture of high craftsmanship and the absolute quality of Gucci products are combined, increasingly, with the principles of economic, social and environmental sustainability. In 2004, Gucci distinguished itself as one of the first companies in its sector to voluntarily set up a process of certification in the field of corporate social responsibility (SA8000) along its entire production chain. Besides the values that the whole world associates unequivocably with Gucci, such as creativity, craftsmanship, absolute quality and Italian craftsmanship, Gucci has always had a responsible attitude towards people, territory, the environment and the community, with particular attention to the value of sustainability. This is demonstrated by the projects which the company takes forward with commitment and passion through the co-ordination of the CSR & Sustainability department.

After 2004, the independent agency Bureau Veritas certified the production chains for leather goods, jewellery, clothing and shoes, as well as the logistics hub. The certification concerns business ethics with respect to people, health and safety in the workplace, rights and equal opportunities for workers, and compliance with international laws and regulations on labour within the Gucci system.

Social responsibility starts with numerous annual inspections of working conditions, and auditing aimed at checking compliance with the principles of sustainability to which the suppliers have signed up. Attention to the rights of people as a fundamental asset has led the company to support the Clean Clothes campaign, by banning the dangerous sandblasting technique used to bleach jeans.

With the objective of promoting worker health and safety, Gucci set up a permanent discussion round table with trade unions and research institutes in order to study alternative technologies. As part of its staff management policies, the company has extended SA8000 certification to its Italian shops, and obtained it for all of them.[12] Furthermore, in order to valorise employee competence and wellbeing, in July 2011 Gucci signed an agreement with trade unions to redesign and enhance welfare policies, and introduce target-based reward schemes. During the same year, social responsibility training activities aimed at all managers and employees were intensified in order to disseminate the culture of sustainability and open new channels of dialogue with all staff.

Every year, the company renews its collaboration with nonprofit organisations, the first of which was UNICEF. Since 2005, this commitment has raised over $12 million for solidarity projects in Africa.

In addition to these activities, in September 2009 Gucci created a Permanent Joint Committee for value chain policies, an agreement signed by Gucci, Confindustria Firenze (the Italian manufacturers' association in Florence), CNA Firenze (the national federation of craft trades) and the trade unions, in order to protect and develop the company's value chain, and more generally the territory of Florence and Tuscany, as a unique heritage of knowledge and values for the country. It is a matter of knowledge and skills which, if dispersed, could never be regained, with irreparable damage not just to Gucci but to the entire industry. The committee's agenda primarily concerns the management of social impacts, the monitoring of environmental impacts, a more responsible use of company input and international solidarity programmes.

---

12   Gucci shops comply with the principles indicated by SA8000, officially defined as a standard 'based on international human rights norms and national labour laws that will protect and empower all personnel within a company's scope of control and influence, who produce products or provide services for that company', thus guaranteeing respect for human and workers' rights, and health and safety in the workplace (www.sa-intl.org/index.cfm?fuseaction=Page.ViewPage&pageId=937).

4.10.2 The Better Cotton Initiative:[13] Ikea

A world leader in the furniture sector, Ikea has considerable experience in the management of environmental and social issues. Attention to sustainability is inherent to the original business model developed by Ingvar Kamprad, the founder of the company, which was an innovative product concept based on flat packaging which improves the efficiency of logistics by reducing the number of shipments and thus carbon dioxide emissions.

The company has developed internal procedures to assess the environmental and social impact of the products (Ikea Sustainability Product Score Card) and has implemented a code of conduct for suppliers' social responsibility (Ikea Way on Purchasing Home Furnishing Products, or Iway). By collaborating with the WWF (World Wild Fund for Nature), Ikea has also developed a pilot project in order to help farmers in Pakistan change the way they cultivate cotton.

Making cotton production more sustainable is a global challenge (see Section 3.1.1). Cotton is probably one of the most important and widespread crops in the world. At the same time, its cultivation and production is responsible for a number of environmental and social issues. On the one hand, irrigation techniques and the inefficient use of pesticides and fertilisers threaten the availability of clean water, the fertility of the soil and biodiversity. On the other hand, the use of pesticides and fertilisers impacts the health of farmers, and this is associated with difficult working conditions (particularly for women) and child labour and forced labour practices. In these conditions, forms of unfair value redistribution add up along the value chain, meaning farmers are put under severe pressure by producers and experience very low remunerations and tight margins.

In 2005, the BCI (Better Cotton Initiative) was set up to tackle these issues with the objective of making 'global cotton production better for the people who produce it, better for the environment it grows in and better for the sector's future'. BCI is a partnership between

13   http://bettercotton.org.

organisations operating along the cotton supply chain and includes farmers, manufacturers, retailers, major brands in the fashion and clothing sector (for example, Adidas, Levi Strauss and H&M), and NGOs like WWF.

When the problem of sustainability in cotton cultivation emerged for Ikea, the company became one of the founding members of the BCI platform. Cotton is the second most important raw material purchased by Ikea after wood. In 2008, the cotton used by Ikea required around 2,890 billion litres of water (equivalent to the drinking water consumed by a country like Sweden for 176 years) and 170 million kg of chemical substances. At the same time, when the company began to tackle the problem there was a knowledge gap: Ikea had no control over the cotton suppliers and the lack of integration in the supply chain made obtaining information about upstream production phases almost impossible. For Ikea, the next step was to launch pilot projects in Pakistan[14] in the districts of Bahawalpur and Yazman in southern Punjab, one of the most important cultivation zones. The area was extremely poor, characterised by the high use of pesticides and inadequate irrigation systems. The general objectives set by Ikea and WWF were:

- To produce cotton with a significant reduction in environmental impact, at a lower cost and improving the quality of the raw material

- To improve the welfare of farmers by increasing their profits

Ikea and WWF also tried to introduce a traceability system along the cotton supply chain. Three years later, the results were impressive: 50% reduction in the use of pesticides, 50% reduction in water consumption and 30% reduction in the use of fertilisers. Equally important were the benefits for the farmers, who saw their gross margins increase by 42%. The pilot project in Pakistan is a milestone for Ikea

---

14   Pakistan is the fourth largest cotton producer in the world after China, India and the United States, accounting for around 8% of global production.

because it succeeded in demonstrating that a more sustainable cotton supply chain can be achieved at a low cost. As a result, the project was extended to other regions in order to increase the share of better cotton, and new projects have been launched in Pakistan and in India, to disseminate 'better management' practices.

The next step for Ikea was to develop a strategy to transform the image of better cotton from a niche to a mainstream product. With the support of BCI and WWF, the company began to develop new knowledge about the cotton supply chain, ranging from suppliers to farmers. In fact, cotton suppliers were reluctant to divulge information on the supply chain for fear of putting their competitive advantage at risk.

In 2009, around 25,000 farmers in Pakistan adopted better management practices. In addition to environmental benefits, the projects have produced economic benefits for the agricultural community (farmers' income has increased by 11%). In 2010, the objective was to extend the project to other 40,000 farmers. A similar initiative was launched in India where this sector absorbs 60 million workers, and 796 farmers obtained impressive results in 2009: 53% reduction in the use of water, 48% reduction in the use of pesticides and 50% reduction in the use of chemical fertilisers. At the end of 2010 around 100,000 farmers were involved in Pakistan and India. Furthermore, Ikea has launched new small-scale projects in China and in Turkey. The objective for 2015 is to use 100% better cotton and alternative environmentally friendly materials for all Ikea products, achieve 100% traceability of the origin of cotton, obtain lower prices, and increase the quality of materials with a lower negative impact on the environment and on people's lives.

References and further reading

Carroll, Archie B. (1991) 'The Pyramid of Corporate Social Responsibility: Toward the Moral Management of Organization Stakeholders', *Business Horizons* 34.4: 39-48.

—— (1994) 'Social Issues in Management Research', *Business and Society* 33.1: 5-29.

Carroll, Archie B., and Buchholtz, Ann K. (2009) *Business and Society: Ethics and Stakeholder Management* (Mason, OH: South-Western Cengage Learning).

Commission of the European Communities (2001) *Green Paper. Promoting a European Framework for Corporate Social Responsibility*, www.csr-in-commerce.eu/data/files/resources/717/com_2001_0366_en.pdf.

—— (2011) *Communication from the Commission to the European Parliament, the Council, the European Economic and Social Committee and the Committee of the Regions: A renewed EU strategy 2011–14 for Corporate Social Responsibility*, http://eur-lex.europa.eu/LexUriServ/LexUriServ.do?uri=COM:2011:0681:FIN:EN:PDF.

Crane, Andrew, and Dirk Matten (2005) *Business Ethics* (Oxford, UK: Oxford University Press).

Devinney, Timothy M. (2009) 'Is the Socially Responsible Corporation a Myth? The Good, the Bad, and the Ugly of Corporate Social Responsibility', *The Academy of Management Perspectives*, May: 44-56.

EABIS (2009) *Sustainable Value EABIS Research Project. Corporate Responsibility, Market Valuation and Measuring the Financial and Non-Financial Performance of the Firm*, www.investorvalue.org/docs/EabisProjectFinal.pdf.

Elkington, John (1997) *Cannibals with Forks: The Triple Bottom Line of 21st Century Business* (Oxford, UK: Capstone Publishing).

Friedman, Milton (1970) 'The Social Responsibility of Business Is To Increase Its Profits', *The New York Times Magazine*, 13 September: 32-3, 122-6.

FTSE (2010) *FTSE4Good Index Series. Inclusion Criteria*, www.ftse.com/Indices/FTSE4Good_Index_Series/Downloads/F4G_Criteria.pdf.

Lunghi, Carla (2012) *Creative evasioni. Manifatture di moda in carcere* (Milan: Franco Angeli).

Lunghi, Carla, and Eugenia Montagni (2007) *La moda della responsabilità* (Milan: Franco Angeli).

5
Fashion and the media

by Francesca Romana Rinaldi and Sissi Semprini[1]

> If you talk to a man in a language he understands, that goes to his head. If you talk to him in his language, that goes to his heart.
>
> Nelson Mandela

5.1 The relationship between fashion and the media

Along with the product and its distribution, communication is one of the three levers which define the placement of a brand. The biggest change in the relationship between fashion and communication in recent years has been the consumer: we have moved from a 'brand-centric' concept to focus on a consumer wanting more direct communication and dialogue with the company. This revolution was inevitable given social networks and increasing transparency thanks to the presence online of company information which might be of interest to the end-consumer.

---

1 Sissi Semprini wrote Sections 5.2.1 and 5.2.2 and collaborated on Sections 5.3.3 and 5.5.

5.2 Communicating responsibility

Communication is a fundamental aspect of corporate responsibility for two main reasons:

- It valorises behaviour and maximises the benefits to be gained from adopting socially responsible strategies and actions in order to establish lasting relationships with stakeholders

- It creates reputation

Communicating CSR is important because, with the input of all stakeholders, it helps to define the company's identity.

CSR communication is often defined simply as the transmission of information about CSR to stakeholders; in reality, it is a much more complex process and requires an understanding of the nature of the stakeholder and the information they need, without neglecting the importance of communication channels. Considering the diverse nature of the stakeholders, who may not all need the same type of information, 'targeting CSR activities to clearly defined market segments may be a superior communication approach to heavily communicating a CSR activity which is not directly relevant to the majority of the public through the mass media' (Pomering and Dolincar 2009). For instance, investors may be interested in financial data and information, while local communities may want to know how a company's actions will impact on their daily life, health and the environment. The company therefore tries to establish relationships with its stakeholders by establishing two-way communication channels, in an attempt to communicate their performance to the outside world, to incorporate the needs and suggestions of both parties and, lastly, to make common and shared choices.

Depending on the stakeholders in question, we may refer to external communication (aimed at consumers, local communities and public administration) to promote, inform and advertise, or internal communication (towards employees/workers, shareholders/investors and suppliers) to educate and inform (Table 5.1). Depending on the

Table 5.1 **The stakeholders of a responsible communication.**

Stakeholder	Main communication media and tools	Purpose of the communication
Consumers/clients	Websites, magazines, brochures, events, social networks	Promote, inform and advertise
Partners/investors	Websites, reports, direct mail	Inform
Employees/workers	Intranet, training courses, manuals and guidelines, corporate magazines, social networks	Train and inform
Suppliers	Codes of conduct, guidelines, training meetings, questionnaires	Train, control and inform
Local communities	Big events, donations, social networks	Promote, inform and advertise
Public administration	Performance updates, reports	Inform

interlocutor, each company prepares a series of different communication tools, sets up separate channels and uses different languages.

The main communication effort is aimed at clients, starting with building websites: communication must be simple, transparent and straightforward. Companies need to demonstrate that they operate within the CSR framework in a serious and practical manner. Many levers are available for this purpose, the most prominent of which is the 'communication' lever. However, it must be emphasised that CSR cannot be reduced to just communication: if this happens, the concept of corporate social responsibility loses its substantial meaning and becomes merely a matter of image.

With the introduction of CSR logic as a corporate culture, the role of communication changes definitively and a new paradigm is born: the company's responsibility is no longer merely focused on producing economic value and protecting its image. When economic responsibility is placed alongside social responsibility, communication leaves the domain of image and purely company–market relations, and enters the more complex domain of company–society relations. The company then begins to look after relations with all of its interlocutors, and seeks to be appreciated for its ability to meet their expectations concerning ethical, social and environmental issues. According to Nicoletta Cerana (2004), the main characteristics of this new paradigm are:

- *Symmetrical communication and listening.* Balancing different interests is the basic element of each CSR communication. Therefore it is a two-way, symmetrical communication, an ongoing dialogue between the company and its stakeholders. Of course it is up to the company to listen carefully to its stakeholders in order to identify the hopes and expectations that, if met, will ensure a dynamic positioning for the company.

- *Systemic approach.* When communicating its CSR initiatives, the firm should address all stakeholders horizontally without excluding anyone. In fact, exclusion could cause serious damage in terms of cost and reputation. The company must establish stable, long-lasting and non-ephemeral relationships with its interlocutors.

- *From target to stakeholder.* A communication that can be defined as socially responsible should not consider its recipients as a 'target' (a term that is still very popular in the advertising world), but as active bearers of interest.

5.2.1 Why communicate responsibility in fashion?

Many smaller companies do not communicate about their responsible entrepreneurship activities. Some don't want to be seen to be 'blowing their own horn' or using it as a cynical marketing ploy. Some think that CSR communications are the exclusive preserve of big corporations. And to others, responsible entrepreneurship is so completely second-nature that it would never occur to them to talk about it. [...] If raising awareness about your responsible entrepreneurship efforts has never been a priority, you might want to reconsider. Letting people know what you

stand for will not only open the door to potential business
benefits for your company; it might even encourage others
to get involved.

(European Commission, Directorate-
General for Enterprise 2005)

It seems that CSR communication is currently treated in fashion as
something separate, far removed from the values that define what a
brand stands for. This phenomenon also appears in other sectors and
so we can presume that, in years to come, there will be an important
improvement in the effectiveness of communicating social and environmental responsibility, hand in hand with changes in CSR business
strategies.

Why do fashion businesses still not communicate their responsible behaviour? Probably because that responsibility is the product of
fear: fear of contamination, of consumption, of increasing or emphasising social differences. Hence, we believe, this resistance to make
responsibility part of a brand's DNA. This fear is associated with
the dread of being open to criticism or attacks from special interest
groups. Such fear runs the risk of overshadowing the opportunity
to assume a role—fundamental today—in guiding change. For the
company, the opportunity is above all one of establishing and maintaining a more authentic relationship with its clients and, in general,
with public opinion: social media is the ideal tool to achieve this goal.

Cultivating and nurturing a brand is an ongoing process which
requires constant attention. If businesses—at least the most innovative ones—are becoming more aware that responsibility is a new and
different way of doing business in order to continue to prosper as
time goes on, then communicating responsibility is an opportunity
to realign reference values with their stakeholders: numerous studies
show that the latter accord increasing emotional and economic value
to individual, social and environmental wellbeing through greater
awareness of consumer choices and lifestyles.

The communication of responsible behaviour creates value for the
company, generating demand, reducing risk and contributing to its

reputation. So, a responsibility programme that is consistent with a brand's positioning creates potential value for the company and the brand itself. The more a company is able to offer and valorise its own responsibility for the attention of financial markets and stakeholders, the lower the risk associated with the company and the better its reputation will be. Having responsible behaviour today means becoming spokespeople for new values and new lifestyles in order to create a valorial universe which, set at the brand's centre, might constitute a possible emotional platform on which to confirm the interest and the loyalty, as well as the relationship of trust with customers and all stakeholders.

Brands in fashion are crucial because of the media attention that they generate: they can then acknowledge their important role as influencers of society. Creating products and services relevant to the neo-consumer, thereby helping them to live more responsibly, means assuming a social spirit and being a positive influence while at the same time increasing demand for the brand and creating value for the company.

5.2.2 Fashion: part of the problem or part of the solution?

Fashion amplifies, identifies and influences the masses. It has the potential to stimulate significant change by inspiring millions of consumers to choose and lead a more sustainable lifestyle. But first of all, fashion—as a sector—should and could intervene to make responsibility 'desirable' by creating the ambition to build a better world.

Especially in Italy, responsibility has been undergoing its own ideological-environmental origins and technical approaches, typified by budgets and reports on sustainability aimed mainly at investors or environmentalists, but not at the end-consumer or public opinion in general. The same applies to the more complex system of certification. In short, responsibility today does not trigger emotions, nor does it make people feel good despite being acknowledged as playing a fundamental role in collective wellbeing. To succeed, ethics and responsibility need to be reconciled with the aesthetics and perception of beauty that accompany the concept of 'well made'. Attention to aesthetics will be crucial for creating innovative projects with which to build stories of responsibility, describe new meanings and prefigure a new future. It's a matter of constructing a new company narrative to attract consensus for guiding the company towards new responsible behaviour as it deals with the environment and every dimension influenced by the fashion company.

So can fashion restore aesthetics to responsibility? Certainly drawing attention to aesthetic responsibility would be a great accelerator and could be the way Italy contributes to a movement that currently lacks a centre or charismatic leader, instead being highly fragmented and driven from the bottom up. Little has been done, even from the point of view of communication, to redevelop the value matrix of responsibility and its impact on lifestyles that are simply smarter, as well as more mindful. When we speak of responsibility we usually mean two things: innovation and creativity on the one hand, quality of life on the other.

Only with a powerful push for innovation and great creativity can we face the challenges placed before us by our era. So, imagining the future for a brand means incorporating responsibility values into its DNA and discovering new opportunities. It means injecting creative thinking and different points of view about the past, which translate into new or renewed products, new packaging designs, new value chains and new consumer services which, in turn, open up new markets, attract new customers and reduce risk throughout the entire value chain and lifetime of the product. The future of communication means creating new content to establish a more authentic relationship with consumers and maintain the brand's promise.

5.2.3 The challenge: how can luxury companies communicate responsibility?

The great challenge of the years to come involves luxury companies: how can we solve the communication paradox which, by definition, must address the elite by contributing to the 'creation of the dream', while at the same time being 'transparent' and telling the story of the product? How can we best use new media and the one-to-one communication of social networks to resolve the trade-off between elitism and democracy?

Lucy Shea is chief executive of the London communication agency Futerra, which specialises in sustainable communication. During an interview she explained that the grounds to affirm that sustainability is becoming a driver of status have existed for some years. Another important point for the luxury companies to reflect on is the importance of showing factual actions in advertising campaigns rather than just the product. Experiential branding is the tool to use. The last element is the behavioural change of the consumer: the final scope of all sustainable branding campaigns is to influence consumers' behaviours.

Luxury brands have a considerable responsibility to make sustainability and responsibility cool. Each brand can create its own language, so long as it does so while affirming that responsible choices in product, distribution and communication strategy can be just as 'beautiful' as conventional ones. Let's consider the example of Karl Lagerfeld: for the fashion show introducing Chanel's spring/summer 2013 collection, he chose to fill the hall of the Grand Palais in Paris with wind turbines and a runway that seemed to be made of solar panels. 'Energy is the most important thing in life,' said Karl to the journalists after the show. It is extremely interesting that a designer like Lagerfeld should decide to put the renewable energy debate on the agenda, drawing public attention to this issue. This shows the enormous potential of the fashion business to contribute to the sustainability of the entire system.

5.3 New languages, content, means and approaches to reinvent the company narrative

The challenges of responsibility, the neo-consumer revolution, digital media and the globalisation of markets have all redefined the rules of communication in the fashion sector. The following sections briefly illustrate this change and provide tools for understanding how to communicate responsibility effectively.

5.3.1 New languages and new content[2]

Consumers are increasingly unfaithful, up-to-date and busy, so the chances of grabbing their attention with an advertisement have declined and continue to reduce drastically year on year (see Section 1.1). It is therefore essential to surprise consumers with language that is direct, synthetic, involving and simple. These are exactly the characteristics of language that should be used on the Internet.

Together with new languages, regardless of medium and communication channel, responsible communication needs new content. Such content can vary but it has three main objectives:

- *Build awareness*. To improve the knowledge of individuals with regards to a problem, or create new knowledge.

- *Change attitudes*. That is to say, ways of thinking and considering a problem. A new attitude can be a prerequisite for changing a behaviour, but does not guarantee that such a change occurs.

- *Change behaviour*. To influence people's actions according to the problem. This is where efforts should be focused to achieve sustainable development goals. However, it is a long-term approach and sometimes requires the commitment of a whole generation.

2   Adapted from United Nations Environment Programme and Futerra (2005).

There are two key points to keep in mind when planning a responsible communication campaign:

- *Providing information is not enough.* Providing information may increase awareness, but it is unlikely to change attitudes or behaviour. Accepting that the public does not react perfectly to information does not mean giving up; instead, it is necessary to use other tools (like videos) to make communication more emotional and involving.

- *Frightening people does not mean involving them.* Fear should be used with caution when communicating about responsibility. Evidence shows that fear often causes apathy, the sensation of not being able to do anything. The tone of voice of the most effective communications about responsibility topics is often funny, aiming for simplicity, and when it is transgressive it always uses irony.

5.3.2 New media

Thanks to new media, brands can ensure a high level of transparency and interaction with consumers by setting the foundations for an authentic relationship. In particular, new media makes it possible to:

- *Make a large quantity of information available about products and brands.* For example, Made-By[3] is a nonprofit organisation which helps fashion companies make their supply chains more transparent.

- *Be transparent when describing the value chain.* With this in mind it is possible to use specific tools such as video interviews (as in the case of the IOU Project)[4] and in-depth product sheets which can be easily and intuitively read by the neo-consumer.

3　www.made-by.org.
4　http://iouproject.com.

An important example is that of People Tree,[5] a sustainable fair trade fashion company originating in Japan which also has headquarters in the United Kingdom. Safia Minney, founder of the brand, entrepreneur and winner of many international awards, decided to illustrate its production chain by means of short video interviews with suppliers.

Trans-media storytelling: online and offline integration and emotional relationship

The concept of 'trans-media storytelling' is intimately associated with the concept of online/offline integration and emotional relationship.

Online and offline integration

Communication budgets are coming round to the idea of new media, starting with SEO (Search Engine Optimisation) and SEM (Search Engine Marketing). The successful brands will be those which manage to seize every opportunity deriving from dialogue using these two channels.

Emotional relationship

Kevin Roberts, worldwide creative director of Saatchi & Saatchi and author of the bestseller *Lovemarks* (Roberts 2005) writes:

> All media will survive, all will be interactive within five years (including newspapers and magazines) and all will need incredible emotions. Winners will deliver seamless sisomo (i.e. sight, sound and motion), world class creative and programming content across TV (preeminently), Internet, Store, Mobile, everywhere. Thirty-second clips to half-hour sitcoms to Hollywood blockbusters, giant plasmas to miniature mobiles, emotional ideas fitted to the screen will win.

According to Roberts, a brand always manages to generate 'love and respect' when it plays with: mystery, not revealing too much of itself

5   www.peopletree.co.uk.

and building timeless storytelling and mythology; sensuality, stimulating the senses; and intimacy, generating empathy, commitment and passion. This type of brand creates a deep relationship based on benefits associated with self-realisation, and this is perfectly consistent with the characteristics of the neo-consumer, increasingly looking for products that say something about their personality. If involved in the co-design processes of product/service, moreover, the neo-consumer will be more inclined to pay attention to the brand and probably remain faithful. If the brand is a 'lovemark' or a lifestyle brand (Saviolo and Marazza 2012), the consumer can even become an 'evangeliser' and talk about this passion to their community of friends.

5.3.3 New approaches

New languages to convey the latest content through new media become effective the moment the approach to communication is changed. The two key concepts to describe this change are 'placing the individual at the centre' and 'merging the Ying and the Yang of communication'.

Placing the individual at the centre

CSR communication can only start with a responsible concept of the company combined with the need to create a new marketing strategy. This need originates from the fact that those who interact with the brand want to be treated like individuals and not as a 'customer' or 'consumer': companies must therefore learn to involve, inspire and motivate them towards responsible behaviour. Nowadays it's the use of smartphones and tablets rather than simple mobile phones which confers the power to change things: with a little organisation, it only takes minutes to declare the death of a product (or a political leader). The challenge for companies is to create real benefits and human values in line with these new desires and new priorities. The future is now, and millions of people are the neo-consumers. These are the people who animate social media.

The new marketing concept is led by democratic consensus: citizens create their own brand and create the demand. So together, responsibility and marketing can change society. Today, the opportunity is to give people the power to feel that they are part of a community. Value is the experience derived from feeling that one is part of something new and which has as its priority the common good. This is the path of collaborating with clients followed by brands like Nike (see Section 4.2), Levi's (Water<Less™ Jeans), Timberland (Earthkeepers Movement) and Patagonia (Common Threads Initiative).

Communicating responsibility: some best practice

Levi's Water<Less™ Jeans

The Water<Less awareness campaign aims to modify consumer behaviour (see Section 3.4.2). The novelty consists in the fact that the company has decided to use effective and emotionally engaging videos and window signs.

Timberland Earthkeepers®

The Earthkeepers line represents best practice for the emotional communication of ecological sustainability for footwear and clothing made using recycled materials (PET, rubber and cotton) and organic cotton. The product is explained to the consumer through a campaign and an interactive card.

Patagonia Common Threads Initiative

The Common Threads Initiative creates awareness for the following behaviours:

- *Reduce.* With tools like the Patagonia Care Guide, the company provides all the necessary advice for post-purchase care of the product and for extending its useful life.

- *Repair*. Despite its high quality, sometimes the product might need to be repaired, maybe as a result of being washed. Patagonia provides a guaranteed repair service both for production faults and for issues arising from wearing the garment.

- *Re-use*. Patagonia undertakes to donate unsold products to charity. The partnership with eBay for the resale of second-hand Patagonia garments is one of the applications of this commitment.

- *Recycle*. Patagonia provides a collection service in shops for garments which have reached the end of their life, with a commitment to recycle the fibre or fabric.

- *Reimagine*. With the consumer, thinking again about production and consumption in order to protect the earth and the water we love.

Source: Company websites.

Merging the Ying and the Yang of communication

Communicating messages of responsibility by traditional techniques and media leads to stagnation. Communication must stimulate people to go beyond the information received; it must feed new experiences and stimulate new thinking. When time is scarce, less information can be managed and communication is the factor that can improve our decisions within minutes. It will therefore be necessary to work in parallel on objectives that seem more distant: to inform and motivate, to innovate and educate through images and words. These are the elements for a new communication of responsibility, with the objective—to quote Mandela—of speaking to people's hearts. In short, companies must develop the ability to tell stories, informing and motivating, educating and offering entertainment, talking and inspiring without making the mistake of thinking that innovation is only digital: actual experience is equally important.

In order for new responsible behaviours to spread, behavioural patterns are needed for inspiration. Such icons can be individuals, brands, neighbours, colleagues, social media friends, politicians or movie stars: these are common examples of new ways of living and consuming (or not consuming). Passion, desire and pathos guide the silent movement of the neo-consumer, who is inspired by new values for which the Internet is the great amplifier. In the expectation that an effective communication of responsibility can be maintained, it goes without saying that fashion can play a crucial role.

5.4 Developing a responsible communication plan

An effective communication strategy is based on some key points:

- Understanding the situation
- Knowing the consumer in question
- Establishing clear and attainable objectives
- Defining the message(s)
- Defining the channel(s)
- Defining the campaign management plan
- Implementing the plan
- Measuring and evaluating the results

The best way to convert ideas into actions is to develop a communication plan. The following basic model shows the different planning phases for any form of communication (Table 5.2). To ensure the best use of the model, the communication plan should be shared between the company and the communications agency which conducts the campaign, and that it is always kept up to date.

Table 5.2 **The phases of the communication plan.**

Phase	Questions	Tips
Understanding the situation	• Have you got a clear idea of the context in which the communication campaign will be implemented? • Have you set the key objectives and the time-frame of reference?	• It is important to start from an analysis of major competitors' benchmarks and from a study of social, environmental, legal and political issues and techniques that could influence the campaign • It is useful to produce a briefing on this phase for the communication agencies
Knowing the consumer in question	• Do you know the consumer you want to talk to? • What motivates this consumer? • What does this consumer read, watch and listen to?	• It is important to segment and categorise the different consumers to whom the campaign is being addressed. The best way to get to know them is by carrying out research (focus groups, telephone surveys, etc.) • Think also about other people who might influence the consumer
Establishing clear and attainable objectives	• Did you set clear and attainable objectives for the campaign?	• It is important to define the main objective: raise awareness, change attitudes or change a behaviour
Defining the message(s)	• Did you establish a central message? • Does the campaign manage to engage the consumer's emotions?	• Testing (focus group) is fundamental in this phase
Defining the channel(s)	• Did you establish the communication channels (traditional media, the Internet, word-of-mouth, etc.)?	• Clearly defining the consumer's profile is essential at this stage
Defining the campaign management plan and implementing it	• Did you involve all stakeholders in the campaign? • Did you create a partnership with NGOs supporting the campaign? • Did you establish a time-line for the campaign and the necessary resources? • Did you develop a project management process? • Who deals with monitoring the results? • What happens in the event of a crisis?	• The involvement of all stakeholders will lead to a more effective outcome for the campaign • Planning the objectives to be attained and when to attain them will enhance the efficacy of the campaign • Defining a budget for the campaign in terms of resources (people, skills, time, materials and financial resources) is fundamental • It is necessary to establish who will monitor the results and how these will be checked • It is also fundamental to prepare a crisis management plan in case something goes wrong

→

Phase	Questions	Tips

Measuring and evaluating the results	• Have you decided how to measure your campaign?
	• Are you receiving feedback from anyone who has seen the campaign?
	• Are you carrying out the assessment reports?
		• There are three different types of metrics:
		  – Process (which messages were communicated, to how many people, where and with what frequency?)
		  – Results (how much did the audience change in terms of awareness, attitudes and behaviours?)
		  – Impact (what impact did the campaign have with respect to the overall target?)
		• To assess audience feedback it is important to go back to the earlier work on consumer segmentation and categorisation. The evaluation can be carried out based on:
		  – Website traffic and online feedback
		  – Participants in events and their quality
		  – Media coverage (for example, through online research)
		  – Opinion polls (for example, level of brand awareness)
		  – Requests for further information relating to the campaign

Source: Adapted from United Nations Environment Programme and Futerra (2005).

5.5 The rules of responsible communication

When we think of a liveable and responsible future we imagine a fantastic scenario comprised of quiet cities full of green spaces, with electric vehicles on the streets and all its energy supplied by the wind or the sun. Cities where we can breathe clean air and socialise, and where the local economy combines technology and labour for the good of all. To communicate responsibility, we need to begin by telling a new story: the future is positive.

1. *Positive messages.* Only positive messages facilitate change. The new story we want to tell must be attractive, involving and above all credible, without relying on old clichés.

2. *Walk the talk.* In other words, 'practise what you preach': behaviour should guide communication, not vice versa.

3. *Transparency.* Brand 'credibility' means 'transparency'. Transparency means having a (single) concept, taking on commitments and objectives and sharing not only the positive outcomes but also the failures. We must not be shy: transparency helps to gain people's trust.

4. *Accessible, synthetic and interactive information.* Transparency also involves the need to offer comprehensive and widespread information. People want to know what lies behind a brand, a product or a company, and what are the implications for their lives. For this reason, information must be widely available whenever and however they choose. The Internet and devices such as smartphones and tablets allow open consultation: content should be devised to be enjoyed and therefore it must be synthetic and interactive.

5. *Credibility.* Information must be visual, tangible and endorsed by a credible third party, such as an NGO or an authoritative certification body (but beware, there are over 800 certifications worldwide). No self-certification or greenwashing; if we adopt an authoritative certification we should talk about it. It is an opportunity. If nothing but branding appears on the packaging, the consumer, in general, does not understand what it is about. Certification or no certification, information must have solid foundations and scientific evidence of what has been done.

6. *Relevance.* We need to know our interlocutors and become important to them. Who do we turn to? Who are they? Are they a niche (often and willingly) or mass-market? But, most of all, what motivates them? 'Green' in itself pays very little. People will continue to choose a product or a service primarily for its performance and quality. The value of responsibility must be incorporated into the DNA of a brand and is a great accelerator; however it remains just one of many reasons to buy. So communication should be able to explain why the value of responsibility is of benefit to the consumer. I buy chocolate

primarily because it is good. If it is mega-sustainable but the flavour is inferior, I leave it on the shelf. Instead, its sustainability should be the foundation for excellent quality.

7. *Storytelling.* This new approach, which moves from 'what' towards 'how' and is based on our shared values and on a relationship, is already being driven by the most innovative brands: by choosing the path of responsibility they demonstrate their competitive advantage by explaining how products are made and how they are brought to market. Furthermore, they also illustrate how the company builds relationships, what responsibility means in the industry and what impact it has on society. Let's take the example of a bottle of wine which talks about its origin, the vines from which the grapes were picked, their cultivation, and the processes of production and tasting. Information should not only enable the product to be choosen or puchased mindfully, but allow the buyer to continue the story with the end-consumer (if the wine is purchased from a restaurateur) or with the other diners (if purchased by the end-consumer in person).

Figure 5.1 **Patagonia's 'Don't buy this jacket' campaign.**

Source: Courtesy of Patagonia.

8. *Courage and innovation.* Courage and innovation are also necessary when communicating responsibility. Courage could mean rejecting commonplace paradigms (as with Patagonia's 2011 invitation to 'not buy', published in *The New York Times* and also in the *Corriere della Sera* at the start of the Christmas shopping period, as seen in Figure 5.1), confronting a crisis with great irony or speaking openly about failures. Finally, use the first person plural rather than singular: not 'I do' but 'We can do it together'.

9. *Simplicity.* Simplify, simplify, simplify. When we talk about emissions, people may not know the difference between grammes and tonnes of carbon dioxide, but everyone knows the consequences of travelling by plane, using a washing machine or making coffee. It is important to translate numbers and complex concepts into simplified examples which everyone can understand.

10. *Emotion.* Communication is more effective if it triggers emotions or creates mental associations for the audience. Videos are the most efficient tool for simple, direct and involving storytelling. Emotion is an integral factor in responsible communication.

References and further reading

Bendell, Jem, and Anthony Kleanthous (2007) *Deeper Luxury Report* (Goldalming, UK: WWF), www.wwf.org.uk/deeperluxury/_downloads/ DeeperluxuryReport.pdf.

Berry, Christopher J. (1994) *The Idea of Luxury: A Conceptual and Historical Investigation* (New York: Cambridge University Press).

Bhattacharya, C.B., and Sankar Sen (2004) 'Doing Better at Doing Good: When, Why, and How Consumers Respond to Corporate Social Initiatives', *California Management Review* 47: 9-24.

Bianchini, Marco (2004) *Perché alle organizzazioni del XXI secolo si chiede di essere socialmente responsabili? In che modo possono realizzare un comportamento etico e come possono comunicarlo?*, www.itconsult.it/knowledge-box/articoli/Articoli/Responsabilità%20sociale.pdf.

Carroll, Archie B. (1991) 'The Pyramid of Corporate Social Responsibility: Toward the Moral Management of Organization Stakeholders', *Business Horizons* 34.4: 39-48.

Cerana, Nicoletta (ed.) (2004) *Comunicare la responsabilità sociale. Teorie, modelli, strumenti e casi d'eccellenza* (Milan: Franco Angeli).

Commission of the European Communities (2001) *Green Paper. Promoting a European Framework for Corporate Social Responsibility*, www.csr-in-commerce.eu/data/files/resources/717/com_2001_0366_en.pdf.

Coombs, W. Timothy, and Sherry J. Holladay (2012) *Managing Corporate Social Responsibility: A Communication Approach* (Chichester, UK: Blackwell).

European Commission, Directorate-General for Enterprise 2005, *A guide to communicating about CSR*, http://ec.europa.eu/enterprise/policies/sustainable-business/files/csr/campaign/documentation/download/guide_en.pdf.

Garzoni, Marina, and Roberto Donà (2008) *Moda & tecnologia* (Milan: Egea).

Molteni, Mario, and Mario Lucchini (2004) *I modelli di responsabilità sociale nelle imprese italiane. Ricerca Unioncamere-ISVI* (Milan: Franco Angeli).

Morsing, Mette (2006) 'Corporate Social Responsibility as Strategic Auto-communication: On the Role of External Stakeholders for Member Identification', *Business Ethics* 15.2: 171-82.

Muzi Falconi, Toni (2005) *Governare le relazioni* (Milan: Il Sole 24 Ore).

Nueno, Jose Luis, and John A. Quelch (1998) 'The Mass Marketing of Luxury', *Business Horizons*, November–December: 61-8.

Okonkwo, Uche (2007) *Luxury Fashion Branding* (New York: Palgrave Macmillan).

Pomering, Alan, and Sara Dolincar (2009) 'Assessing the Prerequisite of Successful CSR Implementation: Are Consumers Aware of CSR Initiatives?', *Journal of Business Ethics* 85: 285-301.

Reina, Davide, and Silvia Vianello (2011) *GreenWebEconomics. La nuova frontiera* (Milan: Egea).

Roberts, Kevin (2005) *Lovemarks. Il futuro oltre i brands* (Milan: Mondadori).

Saviolo, Stefania, and Antonio Marazza (2012) *Lifestyle brand. Le marche che ispirano la nostra vita* (Milan: Rizzoli Etas).

United Nations Environment Programme and Futerra (2005) *Communicating Sustainability. How to Produce Effective Public Campaigns*, www.unep.fr/shared/publications/pdf/DTIx0679xPA-CommunicatingEN.pdf.

Ward, David, and Dario Secondi (2005) *Virtual Branding: Turning a Stone Into a Jewel*, General Economics and Teaching 0507001 EconWPA, http://ideas.repec.org/p/wpa/wuwpgt/0507001.html.

Williams, Cynthia A., and Ruth V. Aguilera (2008) *Corporate Social Responsibility in Comparative Perspective* (Oxford, UK: Oxford University Press).

6

Fashion, art, culture and territory

by Francesca Romana Rinaldi and Nicoletta Giusti[1]

> The Republic promotes the development of culture and scientific and technical research. It protects the landscape and the historical and artistic heritage of the Nation.
>
> Constitution of the Italian Republic, art. 9.

6.1 The relationship between fashion and culture

It is still worthwhile to discuss the relationship between fashion and the world of culture in general, or rather—among the many possible definitions—that world where products are exchanged for symbolic or aesthetic reasons rather than for their usefulness. Is fashion culture? Is fashion a cultural industry? Does fashion make culture?

In a famous article from 1969, the great American sociologist Herbert Blumer says that fashion designers translate modernity into

---

1 Nicoletta Giusti wrote Sections 6.1 and 6.2 (excluding Section 6.2.1) and and Section 6.3 (with Francesca Romana Rinaldi).

clothing designs. Modernity corresponds essentially to what is commonly understood as the 'spirit of the age' in all its expressions—art, literature and political debate—which designers tune in to. The cultural expressions of an era, we could say. The verb that Blumer uses to express this concept, 'tune', evokes the tuning of old radios.

This particular connection between fashion and different expressions of culture was actually perceived by a long series of scholars, as well as by the German philosopher Walter Benjamin. The author of *The Work of Art in the Age of Mechanical Reproduction* (Benjamin 1933) dedicated a series of blazing insights to fashion in his unfinished and posthumous work on Parisian *passages* (Benjamin 1999), one of the most famous of which being about the relationship between fashion and fetishism dubbed the 'sex appeal of the inorganic'. Benjamin synthesises in an incredibly current way—male chauvinism included—the link between fashion and other cultural expressions:

> The most burning *interest of fashion* for the philosopher lies in its extraordinary anticipations. It is known how art is often able to capture, for example in images, the perceptible reality years in advance. It has been possible to see roads and halls glittering with multicoloured lights long before technology did so with luminous advertising and other devices. Certainly the sensitivity for the future of the individual artist far exceeds that of the grand lady. However, fashion is in contact more precisely and constantly with what is to come due to the strength of the incomparable scent which the feminine collective has for that which lies ready in the future. Every season brings some sort of secret flag signals of coming things. The person who understands how to read them would know in advance not only about the new currents of art, but also about new laws, wars, and revolutions. Without any doubt this is the great charm of fashion, but also the difficulty of making it fruitful [...] Fashion anticipates surrealism, actually no, it prepares the ground eternally (Benjamin 1999).

Actually, for evidence of the organic and indispensable bond between fashion and culture, passing through the various worlds of art, it would suffice to mention the amazing variety (in both quality and quantity) of studies, essays and thinking that the whole world of culture has constantly and increasingly devoted to fashion ever since the end of the 19th century.[2] The hierarchy of cultural fields (Bourdieu and Delsault 1975) which classifies some forms of art as legitimate (those totally removed from 'an economic economy', from any apparent utility and from profit) or illegitimate (those with a practical side and consequently a 'disgraceful' relationship with economy and profit) has relegated fashion to an inferior position. So, contemporary art (for example, figurative arts), literature, poetry and music (classical) remain the most noble, as they are apparently free from any utility. However photography, equipped with some utility, starts the list of minor arts followed by (or on a par with) the film industry which introduces mass culture, joining pop to the most important arts, until we come to fashion—the last 'good' one—probably due to the fact that ultimately an outfit is bought and then worn. Architecture enjoys special status as an art which is clearly practical and very useful, but one which has been written down, described and cultivated since antiquity.

Nevertheless, fashion has found its own creative processes, with material and symbolic production and its communication in an explicit, organic and profound relationship with culture and its various expressions.

The cultural field in which this relationship is most evident and well known is that of contemporary art, but literature (Baroncini 2010), cinema and architecture (among the 'legitimate' arts), as well as photography (Muzzarelli 2009) and food (among the 'illegitimate' ones) have also always had a very close relationship with fashion.

It is impossible to give an account of all of the links fashion has and continues to have with the other arts: increasingly, companies that are part of the fashion system more truly belong to other 'worlds of art' (Becker 1982): from photo agencies (like the former Grazia Neri)

2   For a summary, see Giusti (2009a).

to the great restaurants opened by fashion houses in their flagship stores, or in collaboration with stars of international cuisine following the first experience of 'Marino alla Scala' by Trussardi (1995) and 'Emporio Armani Café' in Saint Germain des Près (1998). The actual concept of point of sale in the fashion system followed in the wake of the concept store (10 Corso Como in Milan opened in 1990, Colette in Paris in 1996) but also some of the more innovative multibrand boutiques (Luisa Via Roma in Florence, Penelope in Brescia) nowadays appear quite removed from the stereotypical clothing store and much closer to a place where fashion makes pieces of the contemporary world available to the consumer, after selection by a curator/ dealer. Transported from the sacred context of the museum to the profanity of the boutique, the figure of the 'curator' also allows us to note that fashion creates a relationship with other fields of culture in a great variety of ways: from the museum, as we've seen, through to the temporary exhibition. The fashion company or fashion designer is often the subject of an exhibition, or its financier through foundations (Fondazione Trussardi, Fondazione Furla per l'Arte Contemporanea, Fondazione Prada), through commissions (such as Vanessa Beecroft's performances for Louis Vuitton, and 'capsules' or short movies including Roman Polanski's *A Therapy* presented at the 2012 Cannes Film Festival by Prada) or through actual commercial partnerships (collections which international artists, from Takashi Murakami to Yayoi Kusama, by way of Stephen Sprouse, have all created for Louis Vuitton).

In general, incursions by fashion into the contiguous fields of the arts and culture are therefore so numerous and consistent that it is difficult to really distinguish what is fashion and what are the other cultural experiences. In this chapter we shall focus on some of the experiences, in contemporary art, cinema and other territories, which are relevant to the relationship we want to illustrate.

6.2 Fashion and contemporary art

The relationship between art and fashion, from the point of view of content, has a long history of dialogue and more or less explicit cross-pollination, too often reduced to pointless 'next door neighbour' quarrels which are generically characterised by the (eternal) issue of 'whether clothes are works of art' or the never-ending story of artists who use fashion products and trends and, vice versa, of fashion designers using trends from art or the arts.[3] On the horizon, what Bourdieu and Delsault (1975) calls the 'hierarchy of legitimacy' of artistic fields: a fight for dominance in the respective areas in which fashion, relegated to the minor arts since the 16th century (Muzzarelli 2009), continues to be wracked by a dogged pursuit of legitimacy. In the 17th century, the cost of two paintings by van Dyck was less than the price of a single, albeit richly decorated, garment (Muzzarelli 2011). It is not improbable that the reason for the subsequent downgrading of fashion items lies in their rapid loss of economic value, thanks to the introduction of the idea of the collection by the silk merchants of Lyon, also during the 17th century: in order to gain a competitive advantage over imitators, the merchants of Italian, British and Dutch fabrics began to vary the patterns with the help of skilful designers (Poni 2009). This was the beginning of innovation through design rediscovered many years later thanks to management studies (Verganti 2009).

If the idea of novelty sells a fashion product at a higher price, then the inevitable issue of being out of fashion as soon as the new collections come out results in the unavoidable and tangible loss of value that is clearly visible in the end-of-season sales. That was, at least, until the concept of vintage gained popularity. Now some garments are able to regain their appeal and enter a noble second-hand market because they are considered to be classics, signalling a move from

3   See, for example, Grandi (2003); Svendsen (2004); Giannone and Calefato (2007).

a plain 'symbolic short-cycle object' to an 'unused symbolic object made in antiquity' typical of art (Bourdieu and Delsault 1975). Even if a star system of fashion designers, similar to the worlds of contemporary art and cinema (Morin 1957), has been created by giving value to vintage, it is not yet able to influence the price of the fashion product as we see in contemporary art, where a series of multiple brands—the artist, art merchant and auction houses—gradually increase the value of the work of art, even when it has not become a 'classic' (Thompson 2008). Instead, the price of the seasonal fashion product is dictated by the fashion house and, except for discounts or contingent promotional sales, is not negotiable.

However, the differences end here: contemporary art—with its millionaire artists who express themselves in terms of market share like Jeff Koons, or who in reality run their own workshops where flocks of assistants, *de facto*, produce works based on Andy Warhol's 'Factory' model—is really no different from fashion houses with an art director (for example, Karl Lagerfeld) co-ordinating the design of a great number of collections.

Even the alleged non-reproducibility of art has been supplanted because, from 'ready made' onward, contemporary art has taken control of an almost infinite series of forms of expression that have moved away—not entirely but inexorably—from traditional forms such as painting or sculpture. It is the use of experimental or non-traditional forms of expression which makes it increasingly difficult to draw clear boundaries between fashion and contemporary art, especially when one uses the trends of the other. Nonetheless, the question of legitimacy remains implacably in favour of contemporary art.

Regardless of the fashion product being incorporated or otherwise in the work of art, as, for example, Cindy Sherman with Jean-Paul Gaultier for *Untitled #131* (1983) or in *Prada Marfa* by Michael Elmgreen and Ingar Dragset (2005), or whether performance comes out of the art establishments and occurs where fashion takes place, such as Vanessa Beecroft's performances for Louis Vuitton in 2005 and

2006, no-one questions the fact that the result is a work of art or that its creator can be considered an artist.

It becomes difficult to say that installations which comply with the canons of artistic language and are made in containers created for art, such as those by Issey Miyake from *Making Things* at the Cartier Foundation for Contemporary Art (October 1998–February 1999) through to *The Spirit of Tohoku: 'Clothing' by Issey Miyake* (2011), cannot be called works of art; likewise, conversely, real performances amusingly labelled as 'fashion shows', such as some of John Galliano's shows for Christian Dior or those of Alexander McQueen for Givenchy, or even all of Martin Margiela's productions, at least until the designer became the boss of his own company. In fact, how can we distinguish Maison Martin Margiela's performance at the show for the spring/summer 2000 collection (Paris, 1 October 1999)—accompanied by banquet simulacra, fetishist evocations of stiletto heels, models getting on tables and clothing all in size 74 in protest at the standardisation of the body in the field of fashion—from those of Vanessa Beecroft (*Despair* or *'The Book of Food'*, VB01; *Lottem Kampf mit den Berge*, VB08; *The Banquet at Rivoli Museum*, VB52), very similar in terms of food for thought, expressive styles and polemical objectives?

It is difficult to say if fashion companies are aware of this growing cross-pollination. It is true to say that, since the initial experiences, such as those of the Nicola Trussardi Foundation (1996), the Hugo Boss Prize (1996) and the Furla Award for Contemporary Art (2000), the relationship between fashion and contemporary art has gradually intensified and expanded in the form of collaboration supported by foundations. At present, art/fashion foundations involve all the major fashion and luxury brands from Gucci to Ferragamo, and from the above-mentioned Furla to LVMH. However, the relationship between fashion brands and art is different: it ranges from mere patronage to full commercial partnership. The former is illustrated by Furla, which declares explicitly (see Section 6.4.1) that it does not intend to use the 'the Furla Prize for commercial purposes [...] as a form of direct spillover for their own products';[4] the latter by Louis Vuitton who gets leading artists from the contemporary art world (Murakami, Sprouse, Kusama) to take part in collections by signing them up. An intermediate form of relationship, similar to patronage, can involve sponsorship of single exhibitions (for example, LVMH with exhibitions by Andy Warhol in 2009, Picasso in 2008 or Yves Klein in 2006, or Hugo Boss with the Hans Peter Feldmann exhibition at the Serpentine Gallery in London and the Jeff Koons exhibition at the Beyeler Foundation in Basel, both in 2012) or the realisation of performances/works *in situ*, effectively turning the points of sale into exhibition spaces.

Apparently there is no explanation for why fashion companies are particularly active in the contemporary art sector rather than other cultural fields.

Other experiences bind fashion businesses to music and to the theatre, for example, the Carla Fendi Foundation and the Festival dei Due Mondi [Two Worlds Festival] in Spoleto or the Alda Fendi Foundation and the Rome Film Festival. Historically, the world of fashion became part of culture through music and theatre, as well as through the applied arts: it suffices to mention the example of Diaghilev's Ballets Russes, which managed to involve personalities such as Jean Cocteau, Coco Chanel, Paul Poiret, Pablo Picasso and Igor Stravinsky. In this case, it is impossible to separate the different forms of art from one another. Even the creative vocation of fashion designers expresses itself in different fields: for every Karl Lagerfeld or Hedi Slimane photographer, there is also a Christian Dior composer of *suites françaises* or an Yves Saint Laurent illustrator with his adult comic strip, *La vilaine Lulu*. On the other hand, artists who were already famous in the figurative arts, such as Paul Iribe, Jean Cocteau and Raoul Dufy, willingly lent their brush or pencil to prestigious fashion houses like Chanel or Schiaparelli.[5]

---

4   Source: Interview with Giovanna Furlanetto, president of Furla.
5   For a historical survey of the connections between art and fashion, and between artists and fashion houses, see Giusti (2009a).

It is perhaps when the creative experience uses different forms of expression that we see the true connection between fashion and the other arts. For fashion, the structure of the business is dependent upon looking for novelties and trends, and this search can be mediated by languages belonging to other artistic forms like music, illustration, painting, theatre, contemporary art or the cinema. For example, to prepare a mood board (the board showing trends which comprises the first step for every new collection)[6] the style office gathers a long series of cultural products of various kinds, drawing on different arts and fields of culture, and 'translates' them into the most appropriate medium for fashion, comprising technical drawings and prototypes of clothes, while also using other forms of expression typical of other arts (videos, collage, etc.). The use of 'other' languages, then, implies in some cases that fashion connects with forms of art perceived as more legitimate. This contiguous relationship with contemporary art also creates added value for the fashion house or label. This extra value is evident in the vintage market: as we shall see, one of the factors that determines whether vintage garments increase in price at auctions is the open integration with contemporary art. Thus, the highest value ever achieved by a pre-Second World War garment is a Schiaparelli jacket decorated with a drawing by Jean Cocteau, sold for €175,000 in 2009 (Crane 2011). A 1966 item by Yves Saint Laurent belonging to the famous Mondrian collection was auctioned in London in 2011 for about €35,000. In general, though, vintage items rarely exceed €10,000.

With the progressive legitimisation of fashion houses as patrons or discoverers of talent in art, understanding who legitimises whom is relative: young creative artists 'graduating' from the Furla Award have more rapidly attained the status of artist thanks to this recognition, and with less critical scrutiny than any of their contemporaries who might have been forced to go through the 'usual' gallery channels. Fashion tycoons and fashion designers—especially François

6   For example see Giusti (2009b).

Pinault—are often art collectors and, like all famous collectors, they help push up the price of a work of art when it comes under the hammer (Thompson 2008). The favour is returned. So the problem is not who legitimises whom, but admitting that there is a process for building brand value that is very similar in both fashion and contemporary art (Bourdieu and Delsault 1975; Bourdieu 1977). Fashion businesses, fashion designers and artists are taking up reciprocal positions in their respective fields, becoming important players for building product value for each other thanks to a mutual curiosity triggered by the contiguity of creative languages, and by the similarity in their processes for building a product's value. Not only that: we have already mentioned the mood board, which is a plurality of cultural products used by the fashion designer when starting to develop new fashion products; actually, it is becoming progressively evident that creative processes can be plotted on a straight line which goes from the seemingly least structured proceeses of contemporary art, through areas in which creativity is organised, such as music, literature, fashion and design, to end with technological innovation.[7] Fashion's desire to connect with other expressive forms of culture and creativity, starting with contemporary art, appears on the one hand to be more legitimate, and on the other hand freer, and therefore seems more than understandable, beyond any economic consideration.

Examples of collaboration between fashion and art

Louis Vuitton and Takashi Murakami

> When I first saw Takashi Murakami's work, I smiled and wondered, Where did this explosion come from? [...] there he was, standing in my Paris office, wearing his round, wire-rimmed glasses, skeleton-print T shirt, baggy short pants and a sort of samurai ponytail. He looked like a cool skater kid, an eternal teenager. He and his crew, with total respect for Vuitton's heritage, were eager to contribute to

7   See also Smith (2008).

the creation of a new chapter [in the history of the *maison*]. [...] Our first agreed-upon work was a straightforward interpretation of Vuitton's traditional monogram. What had once been set in brown with gold symbols was now alive in 33 clashing colors against a jet black or optic white background. [In time], each symbol within the monogram would soon have its very own identity (Jacobs 2008).

The icon of elegance and French *art de vivre*, Louis Vuitton has cultivated a close relationship with the world of art since the fashion house was founded in 1854, but it was with the arrival of Marc Jacobs in 1997 that these collaborations intensified and became ever more fundamental to the identity of the brand. Louis Vuitton has collaborated with numerous artists, of whom Takashi Murakami is just one. Murakami is one of the most famous artists on the international scene, so much so that *Time* magazine named him the most influential representative of Japanese contemporary culture in 2008.[8]

The collaboration between Murakami and Louis Vuitton lasted from 2003 until 2010 and was very profitable; moreover, the artist not only provided new designs for the company but also produced works of art, while on the occasion of his 2007–08 retrospective at the MOCA in Los Angeles, Louis Vuitton opened a boutique inside the actual exhibition in order to sell products resulting from its collaboration with the artist.

With such a collaboration, art enters the confines of fashion and fashion trancends those of art. So, should the Louis Vuitton bags he designed acquire the status of works of art? Because, just as Warhol said, the commercial should not necessarily detract from the aesthetic. And because, as Andy Warhol also said, 'Being good in business is the most fascinating kind of art' (Warhol 1975): breaking expectations is how the avant-garde works.

Converse and Damien Hirst

In 2010, Damien Hirst, one of the richest contemporary artists in the world, designed an edition of the Chuck Taylor All Star training shoe for Converse, with blue and yellow butterflies on a red background. The

8   www.time.com/time/specials/packages/completelist/0,29569,1733748,00. html.

→

motif was inspired by Hirst's painting *All You Need Is Love*, which was auctioned at Sotheby's in 2008 for $2,420,000 dollars in aid of the charity (RED). Only 400 pairs were sold (at $100 dollars per pair), with the proceeds used to fight AIDS, tuberculosis and malaria.

The limited edition Damien Hirst All Stars went on sale in Europe in selected shops[9] (Dover Street Market in London, A Cut Above in Antwerp, Colette in Paris, Limited Editions in Barcelona, Precinct 5 in Amsterdam, Slam Jam in Italy and Wood Wood in Berlin) from 5 November 2010, and in America from 1 December 2010.

6.2.1 Differences between fashion and art

If it's true that there are many similarities between fashion and art, it's important to note that there are just as many characteristics which keep these two worlds well apart (Boodro 2011; Stern 2004):

- *Duration.* Art is timeless, fashion is not. Fashion has a short duration, as we learn from its etymological root, and so do its artefacts, the garment and the accessory. Although some fashion designers do use durable materials (for example, plastic for Miyake or metal for Rabanne), fabric remains the preferred material for making clothes and it is subject to wear and tear.

- *Disinterest.* Art has value in itself, while fashion has a commercial purpose. In fact, fashion was industrialised as soon as it was possible to do so, while art continues to maintain, in the majority of its expressions, an artesan quality (Pedroni and Volontè 2012).

- *Authorship.* The artist is considered the sole creator of a work of art and the only individual entitled to recognition. In fashion, a garment's production chain is much longer and many other

9   www.highsnobiety.com/2010/09/28/damien-hirst-x-converse-productred-chuck-taylor-all-star.

people are fundamental to the beauty and success of the final product.

- *Uselessness.* We cannot say that art is useless, but its usefulness is confined to a limited spectrum of factors (aesthetic experience, investment, ostentation, denunciation). Fashion is used to dress oneself in order to conduct a satisfactory social life (Loschek 2009) and is partly bound to specific occasions and functionalities.

- *Uniqueness.* Unlike a garment, every work of art, excluding allographic ones (i.e., those that in order to exist need to be executed by others, such as musical or theatrical works), is a single copy and any reproduction generates a false item.

What distinguishes fashion from art is its predominantly commercial nature, which is a sign of its frivolity and inability to pursue the ideal of *art pour l'art* (Pedroni and Volontè 2012).

6.3 Fashion and cinema

If the relationship between fashion and the contemporary art world, in all its contiguity, tells of an ongoing attempt to establish hierarchies, the world of cinema is freer but no less close. Clothes and films, in the broadest sense ranging from someone's general appearance to video clips, are two means of communication that get along well without any need to prove themselves hierarchically. This may be because they both initially belonged to the 'spurious', minor or recently invented arts, and as such did not need a noble title to contend with each other. For both, this substantial equality in no way diminishes the importance of each medium's power. One of the earliest and fundamental empirical studies—the *Personal Influence* with which sociologists Elihu Katz and Paul L. Lazarsfeld (1955) set the tone for an entire sociology of communication—investigated individual choices concerning cinema and fashion. In fact, few means of communication have been as capable of influencing the collective imagination as cinema, if not for the actual concept of 'star' (Morin 1957) so important for understanding the function of fashion today (Kawamura 2005), as well as that of other economies based on quality (Benamhou 2002). Among the designers who have become celebrities, whose lives and loves end up in the tabloids and whose products become the most diverse (the loves of Marc Jacobs, Coca-Cola for Karl Lagerfeld or Jean-Paul Gaultier), and the celebrities designing lines of clothing and perfumes (from Madonna to John Malkovic), fashion and cinema or fashion and the performing arts form a star system which allows us to understand contemporary mass culture.

If we consider that a garment gains value, not only for the designer but also for the wearer, we understand the importance and the depth of the relationship between cinema and fashion. As the American sociologist Diana Crane points out, the most important factor to influence the price of a vintage garment is the fact that it was owned or worn by a celebrity (Crane 2011), in most cases a movie star. In fact, the auction price for a vintage item of clothing, even one by a famous designer, does not reach the millions of euros or dollars that we see for works of contemporary art, unless it was worn by a celebrity. This was the case for the little black dress designed by Givenchy which Audrey Hepburn wore in *Breakfast At Tiffany's* (Blake Edwards, 1961) or the white dress, by an unknown designer, worn by Marilyn Monroe in *The Seven Year Itch* (Billy Wilder, 1955), which sold for €681,000 and €3.54 million respectively. And very few items of clothing have had the ability to shape the collective imagination like the raincoat worn by Humphrey Bogart in *Casablanca* (Michael Curtiz, 1942), Richard Gere's Armani suit in *American Gigolo* (Paul Schrader, 1980) and, of course, Hepburn's *petite robe noire*, not forgetting the tuxedo worn by Marlene Dietrich in many of von Sternberg's films, the leather jacket and tight-fitting T-shirts worn by Marlon Brando in *On the Waterfront* (Elia Kazan, 1954), or the 'vestaglietta' [house dresses] chosen for Sophia Loren in *Two Women* (Vittorio De Sica, 1960) or *A Special Day* (Ettore Scola, 1977).

The causal path—the garment makes the character and thence the star, or the character and thence star makes the garment—should not be taken for granted. The power of clothes in films is not really just perceived by the public: it is notorious how films (like photography) are one of the principal sources used by designers to create collections (Smith 1989; Giusti 2009b). On mood boards, from which designers draw ideas for new collections, it is not uncommon to find explicit references to more or less cult films which provide, in addition to the general tone, direct inspiration for outfits which, filtered and developed by the designer's personal touch, move from films to collections. It is not difficult, then, to find echoes of Marlene Dietrich, Yves Saint Laurent's avowed muse, in the famous women's tuxedo launched by the Parisian fashion designer in 1966 and made famous by Helmut Newton's photos, nor are the Sicilian atmospheres of *Il Gattopardo* by Luchino Visconti (1963), with costumes by Piero Tosi, unrelated to the baroque lace and bijoux of Dolce and Gabbana. As for the 'vestaglietta' and the complex and extremely intense relationship between cinema and fashion, with cross-references between this garment and the imagination of designers, film-makers and the public, the famous Italian scholar Elda Danese has dedicated a (very interesting) whole book to it (Danese 2008). As ever, Dolce and Gabbana, among many others, show how these cinema–fashion shifts are not one-way but follow a path in which fashion also openly becomes a source of inspiration for cinematographic costume designers: it is difficult to think of *Malèna* (Giuseppe Tornatore, 2000) without also thinking of the fashion duo who have turned Sicily and Monica Bellucci into a kind of trademark, even if the film's costumes were actually designed by Maurizio Millenotti. But some explicit incursions by fashion designers do belong to the history of cinema and fashion: from the costumes worn by Catherine Deneuve in *Belle de jour* (Luis Buñuel, 1967) to Richard Gere's already mentioned Armani outfit, to Jean-Paul Gaultier's costumes for *The Fifth Element* (Luc Besson,

1997) and *The Cook, the Thief, His Wife and Her Lover* by Peter Greenaway (1989). In the latter, the game of allusion between direction and costume is integral to the storytelling: in many scenes the characters, sitting mostly around an immense, Pantagruelian table, are all dressed in the same colour, which is also that of the scene and the general tone of the film at that moment.

Having clarified the bond between fashion and cinema it becomes easy to understand why so many fashion companies have decided to contribute to the cinema. One example of best practice shown by Gucci is its support for independent films and its collaboration with both the Tribeca Film Institute in New York and the Film Foundation—a nonprofit organisation founded by Martin Scorsese in 1990 for protecting and preserving the history of cinema—for the safeguarding of cinematic treasures. Since 2006, Gucci has also committed to adding one restored film to the 'Cinema Visionaries' collection every year, all of which is funded by subsidies to a total of $2 million. In 2011, Gucci set up the 'Gucci Award for Women in Cinema' in collaboration with the Venice International Film Festival. Finally, in 2013, the new Gucci 'Biennale College-Cinema' was born, confirming the fashion house's role as patron to young talent: in collaboration with the Venice Biennale, Gucci set up a workshop for top-level training, research and experimentation for the development and production of audiovisual works produced on micro-budgets, open to directors and producers from all over the world.

6.4 Managing the relationship between fashion, culture and territory

Different examples of corporate best practice show how the relationship between fashion, culture and territory can be managed in a way that is consistent with CSR principles, for the benefit of the artistic community and of the community benefiting from the art itself.

6.4.1 Furla for Art[10]

Furla is a leading Italian brand for bags, footwear and small leather goods. Its interest in art is demonstrated by the Furla Foundation, the 'Furla for Art' project and award and the Talent Hub.

The Furla Foundation is the result of a long cultural and planning process which began in 2000 with the creation of the 'Furla for Art' prize. The foundation was established in 2008, at the instigation of Furla's president Giovanna Furlanetto, to ensure and provide continuity for the company's cultural projects, and to allow them further development and international support. The focus of the Foundation embraces all the creative sectors, from art to fashion design, in support of young talent who are unable to find ways, places and opportunities to emerge.

The 'Furla for Art' project aims to document and support emerging artists by providing a comprehensive overview of contemporary Italian activities, in the multiplicity of languages pertaining to the arts of video, photography, painting, installations, performance and sculpture. The 'Furla for Art' prize was set up in 2000 in collaboration with the Foundation Querini Stampalia in Venezia and the Museum of Modern Art in Bologna (MAMbo), and with the support of the UniCredit Group. The prize was conceived to give greater visibility, valorisation and support to emerging Italian artists.

Dating from 2007, the Talent Hub is a true centre for the promotion of new talents in fashion design. With its establishment, the company changed from purchaser to cultural and social activator, giving young designers the opportunity to put their name, together with the brand, on a collection. The real magical factor for the young talents is actually seeing their bag or shoes showcased in the windows of some of the 300-plus Furla shops worldwide, in exclusive boutiques, in prestigious international department stores, or in editorial pieces in the most influential magazines.

---

10   Source for this section: company documentation and www.fondazionefurla. org.

6.4.2 The Gucci Museum[11]

Gucci decided to endorse its relationship with art by opening a museum inside the historic Palazzo della Mercanzia, in the Piazza della Signoria in Florence, in 2011. Designed by creative director Frida Giannini, the Gucci Museum is a living space encompassing the brand's 'Forever Now' philosophy. The permanent exhibition from the Gucci archives, preserved and expanded in terms of richness and cultural relevance in subsequent years, is situated alongside a series of contemporary art installations selected with backing from the Pinault Foundation. The museum is complemented by shops selling iconic Gucci products and items, a bookstore and a coffee shop.

> Since my first visit to the archive, nine years ago, I felt a profound responsibility towards the brand's legacy. I wanted to bring the precious archive back to life to celebrate the great storytelling power which exists behind the incredible variety of Gucci's products and iconic motifs. I reckoned that this year, the 90th anniversary, was the right time to inaugurate a space where we could reveal our hidden treasures to the public for the first time. In this way, the Gucci Museum not only preserves and celebrates the most significant moments of our history, but also becomes the official witness of its history, evolution and cultural influence (Frida Giannini).

> We decided to give life to a dynamic and involving space. Visitors to the Gucci Museum will not have the impression of looking at a nostalgic celebration; on the contrary, our aim was to offer an experience through which people can appreciate and share our history, understanding, at the same time, that Gucci is still alive and innovative [...] The Gucci Museum is also a tribute to our city. Even if Gucci is indeed an international enterprise, we continue to remain absolutely a Florentine story of success. We owe so much to the ability, the traditions and innovation of our local craftsmen, who represent with pride the values of 'made in

11   Source for this section: company documentation and www.gucci.com/us/ worldofgucci/mosaic/the_house_of_gucci/gucci_museo.

Italy'. We are deeply grateful to the city of Florence for the support that has allowed us to create the museum in such a historically important location in the heart of the city (Patrizio di Marco, president and CEO of Gucci).

6.4.3 The Ferragamo museum[12]

The Salvatore Ferragamo museum, one of the first corporate museums in Italy, is devoted to historicising the activities of Salvatore Ferragamo, archiving and studying his products, particularly his 450 patents, and cataloguing the material in its permanent collection housed in the Palazzo Spini Feroni, where it maintains a rotating exhibition (more than 14,000 pieces have been catalogued and conserved) aimed at both national and international visitors, who for many decades have admired Ferragamo's artistic quality and recognised his leading role in the world of fashion and of aesthetic experimentation.

Since its foundation in 1995, the museum, directed by Stefania Ricci, has organised many cultural initiatives, in particular major exhibitions on the life and activities of Salvatore Ferragamo and on famous film stars such as Greta Garbo, Audrey Hepburn and Marilyn Monroe, all of whom were faithful clients of his. The exhibitions are designed and produced with a dual purpose. First, they tell the story of a man who expressed his artistic talent in the creation of perfect shoes. Second, they demonstrate the spirit of research and innovation which embodies the Ferragamo company, which has always been interested in contemporary phenomena which through art, design, entertainment, costume, communication and information extend its influence on style and on ways of dressing and living.

As confirmation of the institution's cultural value and its many exhibition and training activities, Ferragamo received the prestigious Guggenheim Enterprise and Culture award in 1999, international recognition conferred on the business which has made the most

---

12   Source for this section: interview with Stefania Ricci, director of the Salvatore Ferragamo museum.

significant contribution to the field of culture. For many years now the Salvatore Ferragamo museum has participated in Museimpresa, an association which brings together the most important Italian corporate museums, evidence of a culture of networking and collaboration which has always animated the institution's activities, devoted to a territory overflowing with art, fashion and ancient crafts.

> Salvatore Ferragamo has always been interested in the world of art, not only by mindfully choosing to establish his business in a city like Florence which was the symbol of Italian art and culture in the mid-1920s, but also by making contact with artists, collaborating with them and drawing inspiration from their work. In the 1920s in fact, Ferragamo chose a futurist artist, Lucio Venna, to design his first logo, the label for his shoes and his first advertisements, and then, in the 1950s, he asked Pietro Annigoni to create the graphics for all his business stationery. The work of avant-garde artists like Sonia Delaunay or the cubists, the *fauves* painters, were a continuous source of inspiration. Their acquaintance was possible thanks to the collectors and patrons of these artists who were Ferragamo's customers.[13]

Taking advantage of this DNA, the company has continued to promote, through the institution of the museum, cultural initiatives which are strongly rooted in the history of its own territory. Tradition and innovation are two values of the brand which are reflected in the museum's cultural decisions and the spin it wants to put on its own activities, while also trying to reconnect with the artisan heart of the city.

The main objective of the Salvatore Ferragamo museum is not just to tell the extraordinary story of an entrepreneur and demonstrate the brand values that played an important role in developing 'made in Italy', but also through its activities and cultural initiatives to stimulate reflections which might be useful for maintaining people's well-being, especially for young people in need of examples and points of reference.

13   Source: Company internal documents.

6.4.4 ZegnArt[14]

ZegnArt is the name given to the Ermenegildo Zegna Group's activities in the contemporary cultural arena. It covers all the company's different projects in the field of contemporary visual arts in Italy and abroad, in collaboration with artists, curators and cultural institutions and organisations. Conceived as an independent entity but, at the same time, complementing and continuing the company's activity in a way that is consistent with the family and entrepreneurial traditions that go back to its founder Ermenegildo Zegna, ZegnArt is based upon the company's intense participation in each phase of a project's planning and production, in order to create a virtuous circle capable of forming a meeting point between the two worlds of business and culture.

The project is born out of the Ermenegildo Zegna Group's conviction that investing in culture signifies an investment in the human capital of information and knowledge, in the social capital of relations and trust, and the symbolic capital of identity and recognisability. A tool capable of generating new thought and creating connections and occasions for dialogue with diverse stakeholders, both in and outside the company, in turn producing value in itself and collectively, in Italy and abroad.

ZegnArt is structured into three main areas, each characterised by a specific mission, field of intervention and curatorial framework: 'Public', 'Art in Global Stores' and 'Special Projects'. This three-part structure facilitates the identification of specific aspects in each section, making it easier for the public to understand, highlighting differences between them and returning the group's commitment to the visual arts through a combination of diverse and co-ordinated actions, the expression of a unique and coherent project concept.

14   Source for this section: www.zegnart.com.

6.4.5 Tod's[15]

Tod's dedication to the arts is evident as soon as one enters the company's headquarters, a contemporary white marble building with large windowed façades nestled in the Marche hills near Ancona. It is architecturally unique: a square building with 250,000 m² split over two floors overlooking 65,000 m² of green space. It is enhanced by several pieces of contemporary art including: a unique wave-like staircase at the heart of the building, designed by Ron Arad; rice paper mobiles designed by the Japanese artist Jacob Hashimoto, the most striking being one piece comprised of a thousand kites, handcrafted on site by the artist; huge photographs by Giovanni Gastel; and, in the gardens, a sculpture of a woman's face by Igor Mitoraj.

Tod's contribution to Italian artistic and cultural heritage is characterised by financing the €25 million restoration of the Colosseum (see Section 4.7). The day after the funding's approval, Diego Della Valle, Tod's president, stated:

> Tod's is proud to support this project by contributing to the best preservation of one of Italy's world landmarks and the further dissemination of our culture in an international context. I hope that this operation can promote more tourism in our country, thus creating employment opportunities in a sector in which we are undeniably world leaders, and serve as a stimulus for the many Italian and foreign companies who have the marvels of our artistic heritage at their heart.

Tod's demonstrated its support for cinema with the restoration of the masterpiece *Shoeshine*, directed by the great Vittorio De Sica, one of the cult films of world cinema, while its contribution to the world of ballet is marked by the emotional short film *An Italian Dream*, directed by the German Matthias Zentner and produced by Tod's in partnership with the Teatro alla Scala in 2010. Their collaboration seeks to celebrate the importance of preserving the heritage of Italian craftsmanship.

15   Source for this section: company documentation and www.todsgroup.com.

The fashion and cultural resources of the territory: towards the cultural district[16]

Having clarified the connection that companies could have with art and culture in general, it seems important to analyse how this may be contextualised within a territory. Having an organic relationship with the world of art and culture has a lot to do with the added aesthetic value that is an important part of the value proposition in the fashion world. The *genius loci*, the territory in which the company operates, the landscape and all its natural, environmental as well as cultural resources, are another important source for aesthetic inspiration: the responsible fashion company should feel compelled to return to the territory what it took during the creation phase.

There are several examples of cities (especially Noto, in Sicily) which have tried to create a system for valorising the territory's different actors and resources: the concept of 'cultural district' is increasingly used to refer both to this process and to the end result. By establishing cultural districts it is possible to develop innovative strategies which set in motion the systematic and environmentally friendly valorisation of typical territorial resources. Pietro Valentino defines it as follows:

> The cultural district is a system of relationships that, on the one hand, connects activities for the valorisation of different resources (cultural and environmental, tangible and intangible, reproducible or otherwise) giving life to a meta-process or an integrated valorisation process; on the other hand, it connects this integrated process with the supply of skill, infrastructure and services in the area and with companies which, upstream or downstream, are well matched to valorisation activities. [...] The resources or cultural facilities that can be valorised in the form of a district take different forms as they are made up of: goods and cultural institutions; live events; the production of contemporary art; the film industry; the television industry; the publishing industry; the multimedia industry; typical local products; the fashion and design industry; festivals, and so on (Valentino *et al.* 2003).

16   This section was written by Gaetano Rinaldi, national councillor for Italia Nostra and expert on—and promoter of—cultural districts in Italy.

From an organisational point of view, the form of the district is derived from the world of industry and, specifically, from the concept of an industrial district with which it shares the following characteristics:

- A bond between the product and the land
- The definition of a precise standard of quality for the goods and services which are produced
- An exchange of knowledge, skills and expertise among those working in the value chain
- Production supported by a strong public sector presence

For this reason, the creation of cultural districts is doubly appropriate both within the fashion system and within the Italian system.

An essential prerequisite is a genuine desire to adopt the necessary measures for setting up the districts while taking into account the elements that characterise the philosophy, i.e. the 'protection, preservation and maturation' of the territory's resources. The only condition which can promote these innovative choices by public administrators, with the essential collaboration of companies operating in the territory, is the presence of the 'three Ts' for encouraging the development of the so-called 'creative class' (Florida 2003), i.e. talent, technology and tolerance, to which it would be appropriate to add a fourth 'T' to represent territory.

This process allows the exploitation of the production chain which, by basing supply on local and unique resources, gives itself a competitive advantage over products made by economies with lower production costs. Moreover, we should not forget that image adds value for the district's territory compared to other less valuable realities. The rigorous protection, intelligent preservation, and systematic and eco-friendly maturation of the district's valuable resources allow companies to present them as unrepeatable, unique and precious. Unanimous action by public administrations, various stakeholders and community awareness can also encourage the creation of a seal of overall quality, which confers further value to goods and services produced in the territory. Binding the fashion world to the systematic process of development, starting with the creation of cultural districts, leads to undeniably

→

positive scenarios. Connecting the fashion system to the tradition of places and their natural materials, to forms and artistic expressions developed over the course of centuries of civilisation, and the precious urban environments and enchanting landscapes in which production takes place, helps to enhance the image of the goods produced.

However, connecting the phenomenon of fashion to the cultural context of the territory does not mean referring, in a sterile way, to what has been done in the territory over the course of time. The cultural evolution of places must be preserved with care. In addition, there must be an intelligent reprocessing of stimuli by adapting them to new needs and a renewed sensitivity to new ways of living, involving skilled professions, artists, communities, artisans and companies in this acculturation. Therefore, the importance of the art world in valorising the phenomenon of fashion is understood whether we refer to painters or film-makers and photographers.

It is evident that the ability to bond the image of fashion to the typicality of the territory and its assets—from landscape to enchanting urban centres, the skill of operators or the natural products of the territory, artistic events, the museums and archives which recall the long history that lies behind today's fashion or which extol and ennoble more recent and current productions—represents undeniable added value. Some of the more sensitive and shrewd entrepreneurs have already spotted great potential to be exploited. It suffices to mention here the prestigious activities of Brunello Cucinelli who, in the beautiful context of verdant Umbria creates quality products with a shrewd use of natural materials, with the involvement of sensitive, motivated and properly rewarded collaborators in the production process, with an image that seems at one with the historic urban settlement of an ancient civilisation, and with an intact and enchanting landscape, the medieval village of Solomeo (see Chapter 8).

References and further reading

Allwood, Julian M., Søren Ellebaek Laursen, Cecilia Malvido de Rodríguez and Nancy M.P. Bocken (2006) *Well Dressed?* (Cambridge, UK: University of Cambridge Institute of Manufacturing).

Baroncini, Daniela (2010) *La moda nella letteratura contemporanea* (Milan: Bruno Mondadori).

Becker, Howard S. (1982) *Art Worlds* (Berkeley, CA: University of California Press); Italian translation, *Mondi dell'arte* (Bologna, Italy: il Mulino, 2004).

Benamhou, Françoise (2002) *L'économie du star-system* (Paris: Odile Jacob).

Benjamin, Walter (1933) *Das Kunstwerk im Zeitalter seiner technischen Reiproduziertbarkeit* (Frankfurt am Main, Germany: Suhrkamp); English translation, *The Work of Art in the Age of Mechanical Reproduction* (Turin: Einaudi, 1966).

—— (1999) *The Arcades Project* (Cambridge, MA: Harvard University Press).

Blignaut, Hélène (ed.) (2005) *Anatomia della moda: i corpi, i luoghi, l'arte, il cinema* (Milan: Franco Angeli).

Blignaut, Hélène, and Luisa Ciuni (2009) *La comunicazione della moda: significati e metodologie* (Milan: Franco Angeli).

Blumer, H. (1969) 'Fashion: From Class Differentiation to Collective Selection', *The Sociological Quarterly* 10.3: 275-91.

Boodro, Michael (2011) 'Art and Fashion: A Fine Romance', in Abby Lillethun and Linda Welters (eds.), *The Fashion Reader*, 2nd edn (Oxford, UK, and New York: Berg): 369-73.

Bourdieu, Pierre (1977) 'La production de la croyance. Contribution à une économie des biens symboliques', *Actes de la Recherche en Sciences Sociales* 13: 3-43.

Bourdieu, Pierre, and Yvette Delsault (1975) 'Le couturier et sa griffe, contribution à une théorie de la magie', *Actes de la Recherche en Sciences Sociales* 1: 7-36.

Bovone, Laura, and Lucia Ruggerone (2006) *Che genere di moda?* (Milan: Franco Angeli).

Bucci, Ampelio, Vanni Codeluppi and Mauro Ferraresi (2011) *Il made in Italy. Natura, settori e problemi* (Rome: Carocci).

Calefato, Patrizia (2010) 'Fashion as Cultural Translation: Knowledge, Constrictions and Transgressions on/of the Female Body', *Social Semiotics* 20.4: 343-55.

Calò, Giorgia, and Domenico Scudero (2009) *Moda e arte. Dal decadentismo all'ipermoderno* (Rome: Gangemi).

Corbellini, Erica, and Stefania Saviolo (2004) *La scommessa del made in Italy e il futuro della moda italiana* (Milan: Etas).

Crane, Diana (2011) 'Auction Prices of Fashion Collectibles: What Do They Mean?', *Critical Studies in Fashion and Beauty* 1: 145-50.

Crane, Diana, and Emanuela Mora (2004) *Questioni di moda: classe, genere e identità nell'abbigliamento* (Milan: Franco Angeli).

Curcio, Anna Maria (ed.) (2007) *Sociologia della moda e del lusso* (Milan: Franco Angeli).

Danese, Elda (2008) *La vestaglietta. Una storia tra erotismo e moda* (Venice, Italy: Marsilio).

Florida, Richard (2003) *The Rise of the Creative Class: And How It's Transforming Work, Leisure, Community, and Everyday Life* (New York: Perseus Book Group)

Giannone, Antonella, and Patrizia Calefato (2007) *Manuale di comunicazione, sociologia e cultura della moda*, vol. 5, *Performance* (Rome: Meltemi).

Giusti, Nicoletta (2009a) *Introduzione allo studio della moda* (Bologna, Italy: il Mulino).

—— (2009b) 'Il designer di moda, "man-in-the-middle" e intermediario culturale', *Rassegna Italiana di Sociologia* 4: 579-60.

Goody, Jack (2011) *Rinascimenti. Uno o molti?* (Milan: Donzelli).

Grandi, Silvia (2003) 'Arte e moda: un rapporto in evoluzione', in Paolo Sorcinelli (ed.), *Studiare la moda* (Milan: Bruno Mondadori): 53-60.

Jacobs, Marc (2008) 'Takashi Murakami', *Time*, 12 May 2008, www.time.com/time/specials/2007/article/0,28804,1733748_1733752_1735733,00.html.

Katz, Elihu, and Paul L. Lazarsfeld (1955) *Personal Influence: The Part Played by People in the Flow of Mass Communications* (Glencoe, IL: Free Press).

Kawamura, Yuniya (2005) *Fashion-ology: An Introduction to Fashion Studies* (Oxford, UK: Berg).

Kermol, Enzo (2001) *Cinema, moda, pubblicità: psicosociologia dell'estetica quotidiana* (Milan: Franco Angeli).

Loschek, Ingrid (2009) *When Clothes Become Fashion: Design and Innovation Systems* (Oxford, UK, and New York: Berg).

Lunghi, Carla, and Eugenia Montagni (2007) *La moda della responsabilità* (Milan: Franco Angeli).

Monneyron, Frédéric (2008) *Sociology of Fashion* (Bari and Rome: Laterza).

Mora, Emanuela (2009) *Fare moda. Esperienze di produzione e consumo* (Milan: Bruno Mondadori).

—— (2010) *Geografie della moda* (Milan: Franco Angeli).

Morace, Francesco (2007) *Società felici. La morte del marketing postmoderno e il ritorno dei grandi valori* (Milan: Scheiwiller).

Morin, Edgar (1957) *Les stars* (Paris: Seuil).

Muzzarelli, Federica (2009) *L'immagine del desiderio. Forme e tendenze della fotografia di moda* (Milano: Bruno Mondadori).

Muzzarelli, Maria Giuseppina (2011) *Breve storia della moda in Italia* (Bologna, Italy: il Mulino).

Pedroni, Marco, and Paolo Volontè (eds.) (2012) *Moda e arte* (Milan: Franco Angeli).

Poni, Carlo (2009) *La seta in Italia. Una grande industria prima della rivoluzione industriale* (Bologna, Italy: il Mulino).

Smith, Gaye (1989) *Inspiration and Information: Sources for the Fashion Designer and Historian*, paper presented to the IFLA section of Art Libraries at Paris, August 1989.

Smith, Keri (2008) *How to Be an Explorer of the World. The Portable Life/ Art Museum* (New York: Perigee); Italian translation, *Come diventare esploratore del mondo/dell'arte* (Mantua, Italy: Corraini).

Stern, Radu (2004) *Clothing as Art 1850–1930* (Cambridge, MA: MIT Press).

Svendsen, Lars F.H. (2004) *Mote et filosofisk essay* (Oslo, Norway: Universitetsforlaget).

Thomas, Dana (2007) *Deluxe: How Luxury Lost Its Luster* (London: Penguin).

Thompson, Don (2008) *The $12 Million Stuffed Shark: The Curious Economics of Contemporary Art* (London: Aurum Press).

Valentino, Pietro A., Aldo Musacchio and Francesco Perego (eds.) (2003) *Le trame del territorio* (Milan: Sperling & Kupfer).

Valli, Bernardo, Benedetta Barzini and Patrizia Calefato (eds.) (2003) *Discipline della moda: l'etica dell'apparenza* (Naples: Liguori).

Verganti, Roberto (2009) *Design Driven Innovation. Changing the Rules of Competition by Radically Innovating What Things Mean* (Cambridge, MA: Harvard Business Press).

Vuitton, Louis (2009) *Louis Vuitton: Art, Fashion and Architecture* (New York: Rizzoli International Publications).

Warhol, Andy (1975) *The Philosophy of Andy Warhol (From A to B and Back Again)* (San Diego, CA: Harcourt Brace Jovanovich).

7
Fashion, regulations and institutions

by Paolo Foglia

7.1 The evolution of social and environmental problems from the end of the Multi Fibre Arrangement to the recent crisis

Respecting workers' rights and protecting the environment in the T&A sector should be read as a function of two strongly characteristic factors:

- The complexity of the production chain and the relationships of power within

- The displacement of production towards emerging and developing countries

T&A has an extremely complex and globalised production chain in which the primary agricultural production of natural fibres coexists with delicate chemistry, and the highly intensive production of capital is connected with manufacturing phases which, in effect, have not changed for decades, if not for centuries, and in which the ratio of machine to man remains fixed at 1:1. In a sector which has always been part of human development, the interests and concerns of the big farmer from the US cotton belt accumulate and conflict with those of the small farmer from Burkina Faso, as they do for the large Taiwanese polyester producer and the innovative manufacturer of biodegradable fibres, for the spinner in Smyrna and the weaver living in Prato, and for the producer of an Italian brand and Chinese or Vietnamese contractors.

T&A is also based on a system of international economic relations (value chain) oriented towards export, strongly guided by the buyer (Gereffi and Memedovich 2003) and characterised by a profound asymmetry of power between producers and the global buyers of finished textile products—large distributors and major brands—which play a fundamental role in decentralising production in exporting developing countries. According to Appelbaum and Gereffi (1994), the T&A value chain is organised around five main elements:

- The supply of raw materials, which includes both natural and synthetic fibres

- The production of components, such as yarn and fabrics made by textile companies

- The international network of clothing companies, which includes national and foreign contractors

- The export channels set up by commercial intermediaries

- Distribution and sales networks

Within this framework the activities with the highest added value are not ascribable to production *per se*, but can be identified in the design, brand management and marketing of finished products. These roles are covered by leading companies consisting of large distributors and owners of trademarks which usually subcontract manufacturing processes to global supply networks.

Table 7.1 **Clothing imports: 2000, 2005 and 2007–2010 (billions of US$).**

Country/Region	2000		2005		2007		2008		2009		2010	
	Value	(%)	Value	(%)	Value	(%)	Value	(%)	Value	(%)	Value	(%)
World	208.9		291.2		358.1		375.6		329.8		367.4	
European Union	83.2	39.83	131.5	45.16	165.0	46.08	177.7	47.31	153.1	46.43	154.5	42.05
United States	67.1	32.12	80.1	7.51	84.9	23.71	82.5	21.96	72.1	21.85	81.9	22.30
Japan	19.7	9.43	22.5	7.73	24.0	6.70	25.9	6.90	25.6	7.75	26.9	7.31
Russian Federation	2.7	1.29	7.9	2.71	14.5	4.05	21.4	5.70	7.3	2.20	7.2	1.96
Other	36.2	17.33	49.2	16.90	69.7	19.46	68.1	18.13	71.8	21.78	96.9	26.38

Source: WTO (2011).

The other characterising aspect for T&A is the displacement of production towards emerging and developing countries over the past few years. For a better reading of what has occurred, it is necessary to take into account that the sector's structure was historically shaped by a set of international trade policies which, according to Gereffi and Frederick (2010), have made T&A one of the most protected sectors thanks to various types of interventions: from agricultural subsidies for the production of fibres to the long history of quotas and preferential tariffs under the MFA (Multi Fiber Agreement) which was finally abolished on 1 January 2005. Trade restrictions have led to international fragmentation of the market as a result of some countries reaching the maximum export levels stipulated by quotas and the resulting transfer of production to countries with low labour costs such as Bangladesh, Vietnam and Sri Lanka. In other words, the agreement facilitated the entry of developing countries, with limited technical and economic capacity, into the global clothing supply network.

Since 2005, a radical restructuring of the sector has taken place with complete liberalisation of trade for textile and clothing products, highlighted by two concomitant factors:

- Even if Europe, the United States and Japan remain the major consumers of T&A products, the products sold on these markets are increasingly ones which have been imported.

- The strong increase in international exports has ensured the undisputed predominance of China and the growth in importance of other supplier countries mainly concentrated in Asia.

Table 7.1 shows how imports worldwide generally grew by about 39% from 2000 to 2005, the year in which the MFA was abolished. If we consider individual regions, imports in the Europe Union in the same period showed an increase of 58% compared to 19% for the United States and 14% for Japan. The increase in imports continued steadily until 2008, when the effects of the recent recession were not

Table 7.2 Clothing exports: 2000, 2005 and 2007–2010 (billions of US$).

Country/Region	2000		2005		2007		2008		2009		2010	
	Value	(%)	Value	(%)	Value	(%)	Value	(%)	Value	(%)	Value	(%)
World	197.7		277.1		345.9		363.6		315.5		351.5	
China	36.1	18.26	74.2	26.78	115.5	33.40	120.4	33.11	107.3	34.00	129.8	36.94
European Union	56.2	28.43	85.5	30.86	105.1	30.39	112.4	30.91	98.0	31.05	98.8	28.12
Turkey	6.5	3.29	11.8	4.26	13.9	4.01	13.6	3.74	11.6	3.66	12.8	3.63
Bangladesh	5.1	2.58	6.9	2.49	8.9	2.56	10.9	3.00	12.5	3.97	15.7	4.46
India	6.0	3.03	8.6	3.10	9.8	2.83	10.9	3.00	12.0	3.80	11.2	3.20
Vietnam	—	—	4.7	1.70	7.4	2.14	8.7	2.40	8.5	2.71	10.8	3.08
Indonesia	4.7	2.39	5.0	1.79	5.9	1.70	6.3	1.73	5.9	1.88	6.8	1.94
Mexico	8.6	4.37	7.3	2.64	5.1	1.49	4.9	1.35	4.1	1.30	4.4	1.24
Thailand	3.8	1.90	4.1	1.47	4.1	1.18	4.2	1.17	3.7	1.18	4.3	1.22
United States	8.6	4.35	5.0	1.80	4.3	1.25	4.4	1.22	4.2	1.33	4.7	1.34
Other	62.1	31.40	64.0	23.11	65.9	19.05	66.8	18.37	47.7	15.12	52.1	14.83

Source: WTO (2011).

yet evident. Instead, the crisis exploded in 2009 with a decrease in imports of over 13% in the European Union and 12% in the United States.

The decade under consideration (2000–10) establishes China as the undisputed winner for global exports with an increase of some 260%, moving from representing around 18% of the global market in 2000 to 37% in 2010 (Table 7.2). The same period saw the emergence of Bangladesh, India, Vietnam and Indonesia. The European Union remains substantially stable, while the decline of Mexico and the United States is obvious.

The end of this period saw the final closure of the productive sector in the industrialised countries and regions, and it has now completely disappeared in both the United States and Japan. It does remain in Europe, mainly in the south, where, according to recent statistics (Commission of the European Communities 2011), there were about 202,000 T&A companies in 2008 (11.4% reduction compared with 2005) with 2,100,000 employees (down 19.8% compared with 2005). European companies have had to respond by maintaining the elements which add the greatest value (i.e. design, marketing and the research and development of particular manufacturing processes), by improving quality and especially by outsourcing *basic* production of simple articles with long manufacturing cycles, few colours and few stylistic changes.

7.2 Globalisation and rights

7.2.1 Textile production and working conditions in Export Processing Zones

The overseas outsourcing of production by the manufacturing groups of developed countries and regions matches the interest of developing producer countries in attracting foreign investment by setting up EPZs (Export Processing Zones) (Table 7.3). These take many forms

Tabella 7.3 **The growth of Export Processing Zones.**

	1975	1986	1997	2002	2006
Number of countries with EPZs	25	47	93	116	130
Number of EPZs	79	176	845	3,000	3,500
Workers (millions)	n/a	n/a	22.5	43	66
– of which in China	n/a	n/a	18	30	40

Key: n/a = not available. Source: Egman *et al.* (2007).

including free trade zones, free economic zones, free ports,[1] economic and technological development zones, and the *maquiladoras* of Central America.[2] The ILO defines EPZs as 'industrial zones with special incentives set up to attract foreign investors, in which imported materials undergo some degree of processing before being (re)exported again' (ILO 1998).

EPZs came to the attention of the ILO at the beginning of the 1980s and the *Tripartite Meeting of Export Processing Zone-Operating Countries* report (ILO 1998) observed that in some EPZs the failure to apply labour legislation, the curbing of trade union rights and the absence of workers' organisations highlighted the importance of respect for the fundamental principles and rights of labour. The Committee of Experts on the Application of Conventions and Recommendations (ILO 2003) has noted discrepancies between the ratification of ILO conventions and existing practices in different EPZs with regards to the rights of workers to organise and take part in workers'

1   Defined as 'a geographic area where goods may be landed, handled, manufactured or reconfigured, and reexported without the intervention of the customs authorities' (http://en.wikipedia.org/wiki/Free_trade_zone).
2   *Maquiladoras* are foreign-owned or controlled industrial plants for the processing or assembly of components temporarily exported by more industrialised nations on a duty-free or tax-exempt basis. The assembled or processed products are then exported abroad (http://en.wikipedia.org/wiki/Maquiladora).

organisations[3] (for example, in Bangladesh, the Dominican Republic, Namibia and Pakistan), the right to strike[4] (for example in Panama and Turkey) or the right to collective bargaining (in Bangladesh, the Dominican Republic, Panama and Turkey). In Bangladesh, one of the 'non-fiscal incentives' advertised by the EPZ is 'no trade unions and strikes'.

7.2.2 Wages

Among the factors which have influenced and continue to affect the international process of reorganising T&A production, there is the advantage of outsourcing those stages of the production chain which are characterised by a high intensity of unskilled labour towards countries with an extremely low labour cost (Table 7.4).

In general terms, the ILO data examined and discussed by Keane and Willem te Velde (2008) shows that T&A wages[5] are generally lower than the average salary of various manufacturing sectors, although higher than those seen in agriculture. With respect to this data, it must be emphasised that there are differences in salary between the textile sector and the clothing sector. For example, in Pakistan a textile worker receives almost double the annual pay of a clothing sector worker, and the reason for this lies in the greater technological intensity of the textile industry which requires a somewhat higher level of skill and competence. With regard to actual wages, a survey carried out in some of the largest sportswear-producing countries in the world at the end of 2010

3   The ILO has adopted four important conventions in this area: no. 87/1948 (Freedom of Association and Protection of the Right to Organise), no. 98/1949 (Right to Organise and Collective Bargaining), no. 135/1971 (Workers' Representatives), and no. 154/1981 (Collective Bargaining).

4   The right to strike is not expressly mentioned in any ILO convention, but the Committee on Freedom of Association and other ILO bodies have interpreted all ILO conventions as guaranteeing the right to strike by dint of being one element of freedom of association.

5   The authors consider the ILO data relative to Cambodia, Madagascar, Pakistan, India, El Salvador, Guatemala, the Dominican Republic, China, Mauritius and Mexico.

Table 7.4 **Labour cost per hour in the manufacturing sectors (2008).**

	Country/region	Labour cost including social burdens (US$/hh)
Countries with the lowest labour cost	Bangladesh	0.22
	Cambodia	0.33
	Pakistan	0.37
	Vietnam	0.38
	Sri Lanka	0.43
China	Inland area	0.55–0.80
	Coastal area 2	0.86–0.94
	Coastal area 1	1.08
Other selected countries	Egypt	0.83
	Tunisia	1.68
	South Africa	1.75
	Turkey	2.44
	Brazil	2.57
	Romania	4.03

Source: Jassin-O'Rourke Group (2008).

by the International Textile, Garment and Leather Workers' Federation (ITGLWF 2011) examined working conditions in factories producing goods for major brands and distributors such as Adidas, Dunlop, GAP, Greg Norman, Nike, Speedo, Ralph Lauren and Tommy Hilfiger. From the ITGLWF report it emerges that none of the companies monitored in three countries—Philippines, Indonesia and Sri Lanka—recognise the minimum living wage and many of them do not comply with the minimum legal wage.[6] In addition, the report highlights a gender issue: 76% of the labour force within the survey are women.

6   The minimum wage is defined as the sum paid to a worker for the job or service carried out during a certain period that cannot be reduced neither by individual agreements nor by collective bargaining, which is guaranteed by law and can be fixed to ensure the minimum needs of workers and their families in the light of their country's economic and social conditions. Interest in the minimum wage is based on consideration of the market's capacity to guarantee a fair income to the most vulnerable workers. For many, the minimum wage is a tool to politically redefine socially preferable redistribution of income, and to reduce poverty. Although the objectives of the

Table 7.5 **Female workers in the T&A sector.**

	Country	Female workers (%)
Less developed countries	Bangladesh	90
	Cambodia	90
Low income countries	India	11
Medium-low income countries	Sri Lanka	87
	Philippines	72
	Colombia	62
	Peru	43
Medium-high income countries	Costa Rica	58
	Botswana	80
	Mauritius	67
	Ecuador	56
	Mexico	57

Source: Tran-Nguyen and Beviglia Zampetti (2004).

7.2.3 The T&A sector and gender issues

The T&A sector is distinguished by the strong presence of women, who in the poorer countries have often had no previous income opportunities other than domestic or casual labour. According to the ILO report on the globalisation of T&A (ILO 2005), the presence of women in the textile sector is in line with data for other manufacturing sectors, but is significantly higher in the clothing sector. Table 7.5 shows the percentage of female workers in the T&A sector in selected developing or newly industrialised countries. In general, the percentage of female employment tends to decrease as the average income of the country increases, even if this data is not confirmed in India (where there is lower female participation in the sector at 11%) and in Botswana (where, despite the medium-high level of income, female participation is 80%).

Women represent 90% of the 1.8 million T&A workers in total in Bangladesh. Although the pay they receive is almost double that of

minimum wage are becoming widely accepted, there is still broad disagreement—even denial—about whether this tool is efficient and allows these objectives to be attained.

workers in the agricultural sector, women are often employed in low-skilled production. Tran-Nguyen and Beviglia Zampetti (2004) report that women suffer from discrimination which means they have less chance of promotion to positions for which greater skills are necessary: they are not trained to use new technologies when these are introduced, and they have less access to non-monetary benefits such as healthcare. The ITGLWF (2011) report also criticises more serious cases such as the practice of pregnancy tests before being hired, intimidation or sexual abuse. In the Philippines, in 14% of cases investigated, companies do not comply with legal requirements for maternity leave.

7.3 Codes of conduct and certification

7.3.1 The role of social movements in the spread of codes of conduct and certification

Attention to respect for workers' rights in textile production has developed significantly during the past 15–20 years in response to movements critical of a globalisation which sees multinational companies outsourcing and relocating production to countries which in each case have fewer environmental and social constraints, and lower production costs; this in fact brings about a race to the bottom in which developing countries tend to adopt less stringent regulations and tolerate increasingly lower standards in response to the fear of losing competitiveness in international markets.

In the T&A sector, the pressure of social movements has played an important role in promoting CSR models. As shown by Bartley and Child (2010), in response to the campaigns critical of labour exploitation and relocation which reached their peak in the mid-1990s, T&A companies often adopted internal codes of conduct for the evaluation of supply chains, a practice that also became widespread among companies not directly attacked by activists at the time. Considering the 39 cases where US businesses adopted a code of conduct in the period

Table 7.6 **Social movement pressure as a necessary condition for participation in multi-stakeholder initiatives by 50 leading US companies in the textile, clothing and footwear sector (2001–2004).**

		Enterprises subject to criticism in the 1990s		
		No	Yes	Total
Participation in multi-stakeholder initiatives	**No**	22 (100%)	19 (68%)	41 (82%)
	Yes	0 (0%)	9 (32%)	9 (18%)
	Total	22	28	50

Source: Bartley and Child (2010).

1996–99, most of them (61.5%) had been the subject to criticism, while 38.5% had not been the direct target of social movements.[7]

If social pressure exerted on business is certainly one of the main factors to have favoured the introduction of codes of conduct, it is undoubtedly the lever which also induced various companies to resort to third-party and independent monitoring and certification systems. On this matter, Bartley and Child (2010) indicate that in the period 2001–2004, among the 50 leading American companies in the textile, clothing and footwear sector, only those targeted by activists joined one of the main multi-stakeholder initiatives (Fair Labour Association, Social Accountability International and Ethical Trading Initiative) connected to independent monitoring systems. Table 7.6 shows

---

7   Companies studied in the reputation analysis included: Burlington Industries, Target/Dayton Hudson, Dillards, Federated Department Stores, Fieldcrest Cannon, Gap, Hartmarx, Kmart/Sears Holdings, Kellwood, Limited Brands, Liz Claiborne, May Department Stores, Nike, Nordstrom, JC Penney, Reebok, Russell, Sara Lee, Sears, Roebuck, Springs Industries, UNIFI, VF, TJX, Walmart, Leslie Fay, Crystal Brands, Fruit of the Loom, Saks, Warnaco, Levi Strauss, Cone Mills, Jones Apparel, Westpoint Stevens, Costco and Polo Ralph Lauren.

how social pressure has been a necessary factor in encouraging many companies to move towards verified social responsibility models.

7.3.2 Business codes of conduct

Since the 1970s, marked by further reduction in customs barriers, incorporation of new countries into the global economy and a rapid increase in foreign and multinational investment, there has been a rise in public interest towards the work of transnational companies—especially in developing countries—and with this an increase in requests for the introduction of mechanisms which allow some form of intervention in unregulated international activities. These requests are quickly ratified by various governmental agencies such as the ILO, which in 1977 adopted the Tripartite Declaration of Principles concerning Multinational Enterprises and Social Policy (better known as the Tripartite Declaration),[8] and the OECD (Organisation for Economic Co-operation and Development), which in 1976 intervened in this matter by adopting the Declaration on International Investment and Multinational Enterprises, subsequently revised in 2000.

However, these interventions have had little impact. The OECD statement, far from being a genuine attempt to control transnational companies, was just a mechanism which, through the recommendation to adhere 'voluntarily' to guidelines for multinational companies, attempted to answer criticism coming mainly from the world's southern countries. Even the ILO declaration—more restrictive compared with the OECD guidelines and focused on the social aspects of multinational company activity—is not binding and observance of its principles is only voluntary. Any disputes are forwarded to the appropriate Committee on Multinational Enterprises which express themselves through 'interpretations' of the declaration. Considering the fact that, according to the sixth survey on the implementation of

8   The ILO Tripartite Declaration applies globally to governments, transnational firms, entrepreneurs and workers.

the convention, five interpretations were discussed, it is clear that the impact of the ILO declaration is actually quite limited.

In this context the UN Global Compact is absolutely important. Proposed in 1999 by the then president of the UN, Kofi Annan, as a global system for business and entrepreneurial forces, the initiative was divided into nine points: two on human rights, four on principles of labour management, and three on the environment. The Global Compact is intended to promote the adoption of policies to:

- Support and respect the protection of human rights in the company's sphere of influence

- Ensure that companies are not complicit in human rights abuses

- Uphold freedom of association and the effective recognition of the right to collective bargaining

- Eliminate all forms of forced and compulsory labour

- Effectively abolish child labour

- Eliminate discrimination in employment and occupation

- Support a precautionary approach to environmental challenges

- Undertake initiatives to promote greater environmental responsibility

- Encourage the development and diffusion of environmentally friendly technologies

The content of the codes

Also in the 1970s, the practice of adopting specific 'codes of conduct' began to spread among companies, initially related especially to issues connected to corruption. After a period of relative stagnation, they began to spread again in the 1990s as the result of a new wave of social movements criticising the work of multinationals. In this second phase the nature of the codes of conduct and the scope of their application was extended to environmental and social aspects.

Of the 246 codes catalogued and analysed by the OECD (2001a) 59% concerned the environment, over 60% the improvement of working conditions, 48% consumer protection and only 23% concerned corruption. Of the codes under examination, 37 related to the T&A sector and, although with some variation, all included aspects specifically related to labour.

To understand the content of these codes it is necessary to consider that they mainly represent, at least in part, a response to campaigns promoted by NGOs or governments for the improvement of working conditions in T&A subcontracting. In fact, 41% of the codes introduced obligations or criteria for subcontractors and other suppliers on issues relating to the prohibition of forced labour (39% of cases) and of child labour (43%), extension of and respect for working hours (32%), adequacy of salaries (45%) and health and safety in the working environment (76%).

Application and monitoring

In addition to the extension of the criteria, there are at least two other important aspects to consider when assessing the potential impact of business codes of conduct: measures for the application of the codes, and monitoring.

In order for a code of conduct to reasonably lead to real results it must ensure that companies enforce specific actions, such as: the adoption of a clear policy signed by the company management; the allocation of organisational and economic resources; measures for the training and involvement of workers; the development of monitoring tools; provision for corrective actions; and plans for staff training. A survey by Urminsky (2001) reports that very often the means of application lacked the appropriate resources, adequate worker participation, and transparency. In the OECD survey (2001b) of 118 separate codes, the same conclusion was reached regarding 22 codes which defined criteria for commercial partners (mainly suppliers and contractors), and 96 codes in which the requirements related directly to the organisation and policies of the subscribing companies. Of the latter, only 32% provided for implementation management measures that ranged from nominating a person in charge of the implementation of manuals and procedures, to the verification of economic and financial data. The monitoring actions were almost all internal, and only in two cases was testing by a third party provided for.

With regard to codes referring to the supply chain, the OECD survey highlights a wide range of implementation measures but the most frequent (73%) were those involving sanctions (mainly contract termination) for cases of infringement. Only 23% of the codes of conduct for suppliers expected monitoring by independent bodies, although their effective implementation remained uncertain as far as the right to carry it out was concerned.

In general, as observed by Jenkins (2001), among the greater limitations of the codes of conduct there is the lack of an independent monitoring system to ensure that these tools are not just general statements about principles of business ethics. A survey carried out on 132 codes (Kolk *et al.* 1999) reached the same conclusions. Monitoring was not mentioned in 41% of cases, while another 44% contemplated internal audits. Less than 10% of the codes arranged by companies and 5% of those applicable to business groups or associations had an external monitoring system.

The reluctance by many firms to provide independent audits as an integral part of their own codes of conduct leaves room for criticism that they are more of a public relations exercise than actual attempts to improve sustainability and performance (Jenkins 2001).

7.3.3 Collective corporate codes and multi-stakeholder initiatives

Today, corporate codes of conduct are placed alongside programmes developed by business associations, as well as some initiatives promoted by NGOs which envisage the simultaneous participation of various stakeholders to increase authority and independence. What follows is an introduction to the BSCI (Business Social Compliance Initiative) and ETI (Ethical Trading Initiative).

Business Social Compliance Initiative

The BSCI is an initiative promoted by the Foreign Trade Association—an association which represents European commercial companies and importers at the European Commission—in order to develop tools and procedures for the joint European Business Social Compliance Programme. The BSCI code of conduct, directed at the supply chain, was defined and developed in agreement with the principal international guidelines on CSR including the ILO conventions, the universal declaration of human rights of the UN, the UN conventions on the rights of children and the elimination of all forms of discrimination against women, the Global Compact and the OECD guidelines for multinational firms. The objectives pursued through the BSCI code are diverse and extend to:

- Improving social standards in supplier countries

- Improving public and internal credibility by establishing a transparent interface system between companies, employees' representatives, NGOs and other civic groups

- Providing a feasible and enforceable monitoring system at an international level

- Providing an economic advantage to suppliers and reselling companies, thanks to a common monitoring system for social standards which should allow multiple and redundant auditing to be avoided

Implementation of the BSCI code is based on a gradual approach directed towards improvement which also takes into account conditions for the development of each individual supplier and of the countries in which it operates. The code provides a monitoring system with verification bodies accredited by the Social Accountability

Figure 7.1 **Distribution of BSCI auditing in 2010.**

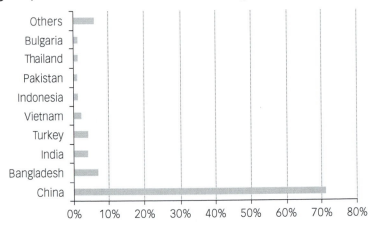

Source: BSCI (2010).

Accreditation Services and for which SA8000 certification is recognised as equivalent.[9] The BSCI currently authorises 16 certification bodies and 950 qualified auditors to conduct auditing of suppliers. By the end of 2010, 644 firms with a combined turnover of over €480 billion and a combined workforce of more than 1.7 million direct workers had adhered to the BSCI (BSCI 2010) and about 7,000 audits had been conducted, including 3,455 first checks and 3,521 subsequent surveillance verifications mainly concentrated in the non-food sector in China (Fig. 7.1).

Ethical Trading Initiative

The ETI is an alliance between firms, NGOs and trade unions launched in 1998 in the United Kingdom in order to promote the improvement of working conditions in the supply chain. As with the BSCI, the code of conduct drawn up by the ETI[10] is also based on the

9   For SA8000-certified supplying companies (see Section 7.3.4), further auditing is unnecessary.
10   www.ethicaltrade.org/eti-base-code.

main international conventions and declarations on human rights and the rights of workers.

By the end of 2010, 75 companies with a combined turnover of €150 billion had joined, together with nine trade union organisations—including the Council of Global Union, which includes the ITGLWF—and 15 NGOs ranging from international charitable organisations such as Oxfam to organisations specialising in workers' rights issues such as Anti-Slavery International and Homeworkers Worldwide, and fair trade organisations such as the Fairtrade Foundation and Traidcraft.

The ETI system for application and monitoring differs substantially from normal approaches based on the certification of suppliers, and does not provide for assigning any label or logo to endorse good business performance. The intention of ETI is to encourage participating firms to incorporate an ethical approach into all their routine activities through the continuous and systematic involvement of workers and their unions in both the measures of adoption of the code's provisions and in the monitoring.

7.3.4 Social certification in the T&A sector

Today, the three most popular certification programmes are: WRAP (Worldwide Responsible Apparel Production), SA8000 (Social Accountability 8000) and GOTS (Global Organic Textile Standard). The following paragraphs are a brief introduction, while Table 7.7 summarises the fields of application.

With regards to social criteria, the certification standards under consideration provide for the assessment and verification of compliance with the enforced law or with the ILO conventions if these include greater protection for workers. The most important differences concern the sphere of environmental protection: Table 7.7 shows that the SA8000 standard does not make environmental requirements, while the WRAP standard is limited to highlighting compliance with legislation and with the sector's regulations. GOTS, unlike the other two

Table 7.7 **Comparison of standards based on their field of application.**

Thematic area	Criteria	Standard		
		WRAP	**SA8000**	**GOTS**
Workers' rights	Compliance with the legislation in the workplace	Principle 1	Section II	Section 3.9
	Prohibition of forced labour	Principle 2	Section 2	Section 3.2
	Prohibition of child labour	Principle 3	Section 1	Section 3.5
	Prohibition of abuse and harassment	Principle 4	Section 5	Section 3.10
	Remuneration	Principle 5	Section 8	Section 3.6
	Working hours	Principle 6	Section 7	Section 3.7
	Prohibition of discrimination	Principle 7	Section 5	Section 3.8
	Health and safety in workplaces	Principle 8	Section 3	Section 3.4
	Freedom of association and right to collective bargaining	Principle 9	Section 4	Section 3.3
	Disciplinary procedures	Principle 4	Section 6	Section 3.6
Customs	Compliance with customs norms with particular reference to illegal imports	Principle 11		
Safety	Safety procedure for smuggling, introduction of drugs, explosives, etc.	Principle 12		
Environment	Compliance with the enforced environmental norm	Principle 10		Section 2.4.10
	Reduction of impact in the production of natural fibres			Section 2.1
	Environmental assessment of chemical products used for manufacturing processes			Section 2.3
	Environmental criteria for specific manufacturing processes			Section 2.4
Composition	Criteria for the composition of manufactured textile products			Section 2.2.
Traceability	Identification and traceability			Sections 2.4.1 and 2.4.13

standards, emphasises environmental issues by providing requirements for the evaluation and approval of chemical products by dint
of their toxicological and ecotoxicological characteristics, and by
introducing requirements for the management of manufacturing processes. Another aspect that distinguishes GOTS is the prescription of
the traceability of raw materials, part-processed goods and finished
products; in fact, it provides for the application of a system to guarantee that all textile products are actually made with natural fibres
produced by organic methods.

Worldwide Responsible Apparel Production

WRAP is an international organisation for the social certification
of companies in accordance with its own standard. The programme
mainly addresses clothing and footwear and is based on 12 principles
which regulate workplaces and the rights of workers, the environment and aspects of security, in keeping with ILO conventions and
recommendations. The standard also extends to environmental and
security issues for exports to the United States in accordance with

Figure 7.2 **Distribution of WRAP-certified companies in 2011.**

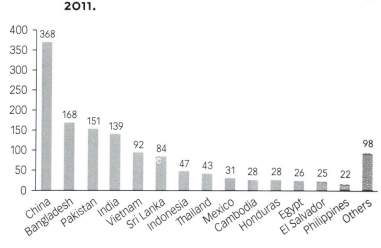

Source: Our analysis of WRAP data.

the C-TPAT (Customs-Trade Partnership Against Terrorism) and the security criteria of the US Department of Homeland Security.

WRAP is one of the most popular programmes at an international level and relies on the support of the International Apparel Federation and 20 business associations in various countries. By 2011 there were 1,350 certified firms in over 30 countries (Fig. 7.2), of which 85% were located in Asia with a strong presence in China (27%), Bangladesh (12%), Pakistan (11%), India (10%) and Vietnam (7%).

With regards to the process of certification, the WRAP scheme provides a initial self-assessment carried out according to a reference manual. In this phase, companies must adopt WRAP principles and prepare documentation for internal management procedures. After self-assessment, the company requests verification by one of the WRAP-accredited and authorised inspection bodies.

Social Accountability 8000

In 1997, Social Accountability International—an international multi-stakeholder association dedicated to the improvement of conditions in the workplace and in the community—created SA8000 (Social Accountability 8000), a voluntary standard which defines the requirements that employers must meet in the workplace in keeping with enforced national legislation, ILO and UN conventions, the universal declaration of human rights and the UN convention on the rights of children. The standard provides certification for companies which adopt a management model and practices in compliance with the following areas: child labour, forced and compulsory labour, health and safety, freedom of association and the right to collective bargaining, discrimination, disciplinary procedures, working time and remuneration.

As of 2011 there were around 2,900 certified production plants in 62 countries, with a combined total of over 1.6 million direct workers. T&A firms are the most represented: 454 in the clothing sector (around 240,000 people) and 312 in textiles (around 182,000 people). In terms of geographical distribution, unlike other programmes in which certified companies are generally concentrated in the major developing countries, SA800 has been broadly applied in Europe where there are over 1,300 companies (equal to 45% of the total), of which 883 are located in Italy (the highest number worldwide and 30% of the total) and 241 in Romania (8.3%). The Italian figures are clearly attributable to awareness programes set up in many regions, in which Tuscany has played a leading role.

Global Organic Textile Standard

GOTS is a standard focused on the promotion of T&A products made from natural organic fibres. Adopted in July 2006 to harmonise a series of standards and textile regulations that existed in various European countries and in the United States, it is based on four principles: the production of natural fibres in keeping with the criteria defined by organic agriculture regulations;[11] reduction of the environmental impact of manufacturing processes; respect for social criteria defined in keeping with the ILO conventions; and the traceability of raw materials, part-processed goods and finished products along the production chain.

Since 2006, the number of T&A companies certified internationally has grown exponentially, increasing from 26 to around 1,500 by the end of 2011. If we then consider verified production plants, adding up all the production plants involved in manufacture for each certified firm including subcontracting firms, the total number exceeds 2,700 plants.

In addition to the global numbers, it is interesting to observe the geographical distribution of certified firms. Figure 7.3 shows that 50% of certified manufacturing companies are located in Asia with

11 These include: EC Regulation 834/2007 on organic production and the labelling of organic products, which replaced the previous Regulation 2092/1991; the National Organic Program enforced in the United States and promulgated as federal legislation in 2002; and the National Programme for Organic Production adopted by India in 2000.

Figure 7.3 **GOTS certified companies at the end of 2011:
distribution by main countries and regions.**

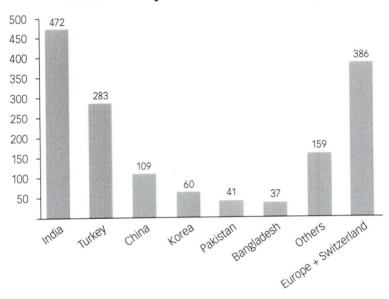

Source: ICEA analysis of Global Standard data.

30.5% in India and 7% in China. Europe, including Switzerland, is
the second highest region overall (386 certified companies, equal to
25% of the total). Another important country is Turkey which, with
283 companies, represents over 18% of the total certified companies
compliant with GOTS.

References and further reading

Appelbaum, Richard P., and Gary Gereffi (1994) 'Power and Profits in the Apparel Commodity Chain', in Edna Bonacich, Lucie Cheng, Norma Chinchilla, Nora Hamilton and Paul Ong (eds.), *Global Production: The Apparel Industry in the Pacific Rim* (Philadelphia, PA: Temple University Press).

Bartley, Tim, and Curtis Child (2010) *Shaming the Corporation: Social Movement Pressure and Corporate Social Responsibility*, paper presented at the Oliver E. Williamson Seminar on Institutional Analysis, 18 February 2010, http://businessinnovation.berkeley.edu/WilliamsonSeminar/bartley021810.pdf.

BSCI (2010) *Tackling the Challenges of Responsible Sourcing. Annual Report 2010*, www.bsci-intl.org/resources/annual-report-bsci.

Commission of the European Communities (2011) *Statistics on Textiles and Clothing*, http://ec.europa.eu/enterprise/sectors/textiles/statistics/index_en.htm.

Egman, Michael, Osamu Onodera and Enrico Pinali (2007) *Export Processing Zones: Past and Future Role in Trade and Development*, OECD Trade Policy Working Papers No. 53, http://search.oecd.org/officialdocuments/displaydocumentpdf/?cote=TD/TC/WP(2006)39/FINAL&docLanguage=En.

Gereffi, Gary, and Stacey Frederick (2010) *The Global Apparel Value Chain, Trade and Crisis: Challenges and Opportunities for Developing Countries* (Washington, DC: The World Bank), www-wds.worldbank.org/external/default/WDSContentServer/IW3P/IB/2010/04/27/000158349_2 0100427111841/Rendered/PDF/WPS5281.pdf.

Gereffi, Gary, and Olga Memedovich (2003) *The Global Apparel Value Chain: What Prospects for Upgrading by Developing Countries* (Vienna, Austria: UNIDO), www.unido.org/fileadmin/media/documents/pdf/Services_Modules/Apparel_Value_Chain.pdf.

ILO (International Labour Organization) (1998) *Labour and Social Issues Relating to Export Processing Zones. Report at Discussion at the Tripartite Meeting of Export Processing Zone-Operating Countries* (Geneva, Switzerland: ILO).

—— (2003) *Employment and Social Policy in Respect of Export Processing Zones (EPZs)* (Geneva, Switzerland: ILO).

—— (2005) *Promoting Fair Globalisation in Textiles and Clothing in a Post-MFA Environment. Report for Discussion at the Tripartite Meeting on Promoting Fair Globalisation in Textiles and Clothing in a Post-MFA Environment* (Geneva, Switzerland: ILO)

ITGLWF (International Textile, Garment and Leather Workers' Federation) (2011) *An Overview of Working Conditions in Sportswear Factories in Indonesia, Sri Lanka & the Philippines*, www.ituc-csi.org/itglwf-report-an-overview-of?lang=en.

Jassin-O'Rourke Group (2008) *Global Apparel Manufacturing Labor Cost Analysis 2008*, www.textileconnect.com/documents/resources/GlobalApparel-LaborCostSummary2008.pdf.

Jenkins, Rhys (2001) *Corporate Codes of Conduct. Self-Regulation in a Global Economy. Technology, Business and Society Programme Paper Number 2* (Geneva, Switzerland: UNRISD).

Keane, Jodie, and Dirk Willem te Velde (2008) *The Role of Textile and Clothing Industries in Growth and Development Strategies*, Investment and Growth Program, Overseas Development Institute, www.odi.org.uk/sites/odi.org.uk/files/odi-assets/publications-opinion-files/3361.pdf.

Kolk, Ans, Rob Van Tulder and Carlijn Welters (1999) 'International Codes of Conduct and Corporate Social Responsibility: Can Transnational Corporations Regulate Themselves?', *Transnational Corporations* 8.1, http://papers.ssrn.com/sol3/papers.cfm?abstract_id=182830.

OECD (2001a) *Codes of Conduct. An Expanded Review of their Contents* (Paris: OECD Working Party of the Trade Committee).

—— (2001b) *Corporate Responsibility: Results of a Fact-Finding Mission on Private Initiatives. Working Papers on International Investment Number 2001/2*, www.oecd.org/dataoecd/45/28/1922698.pdf.

Tran-Nguyen, Anh-Nga, and Americo Beviglia Zampetti (eds.) (2004) *Trade and Gender: Opportunities and Challenges for Developing Countries* (New York and Geneva, Switzerland: UN Inter-Agency Network on Women and Gender Equality Task Force on Gender and Trade), www.unctad.org/en/docs/edm20042_en.pdf.

Urminsky, Michael (ed.) (2001) *Self-Regulation in the Workplace: Codes of Conduct, Social Labeling and Socially Responsible Investment. Management and Corporate Citizenship Working Paper no. 1* (Geneva, Switzerland: ILO).

WTO (2011) *Time Series on International Trade*, http://stat.wto.org/Home/WSDBHome.aspx.

8

Brunello Cucinelli: an ethical and humanistic company

The group works according to an ethical, humanist-inspired entrepreneurial model based on values such as the dignity of people and the dignity of work, which allows it to successfully combine efficient business practices with its social mission. Great attention paid to the quality of life and the human capital of the company, support of socio-economic development, and a respect of and integration with the local area are aspects that have distinguished the company's growth and increased the brand's distinctiveness and recognition.[1]

Far from ostentatious and designed on a solid foundation of tradition and high-quality artisan manufacturing, Brunello Cucinelli products are the epitome of 'essential luxury', embedded in the core essentials of daily life, simplicity and existence. The entire collections are the expression of a contemporary 'art of living', in which aesthetic and hedonistic values are expressed through an elegant and modest attitude, an intimate pursuit of the eternal value of simplicity.[2]

1 http://investor.brunellocucinelli.com/eng/company-profile/profile/.
2 Prospectus for admission to the stock market, April 2012.

8.1 Origins

The origins of the company date back to 1978, when Brunello Cucinelli (Fig. 8.1) started his first cashmere knitwear workshop in Ellera di Corciano, in the province of Perugia. In a district dedicated to hosiery—thanks to the presence of Luisa Spagnoli and various specialist *façonisti* (garment assembly subcontractors) and suppliers—Brunello understood that coloured cashmere could be an important innovation, especially for a female audience. Until then, cashmere had been exclusively produced in natural colours and mainly intended for the menswear market.

> I had observed one of my young fellow countrymen, another entrepreneur, Luciano Benetton, who had achieved unprecedented success with colourful sweaters. I thought that what Benetton had done with pure virgin wool could be done with cashmere as well. So I went out and looked for an old acquaintance in my town, a knitwear manufacturer,

Figure 8.1 **Brunello Cucinelli.**

Source: Courtesy of the Brunello Cucinelli company.

and asked him to sell me a few kilos of that precious yarn, and with a couple of skilled knitters we began creating the first sweater for women, with slightly different shapes: new garments, a little bit longer and fitted but, most of all, colourful. It was the first collection: five sweaters in all, in different colours. I loaded them onto a van and left at night for Trentino Alto Adige—where I had been told that shopkeepers paid promptly—and I returned home with the first order for 53 sweaters. This is the beginning of our story (Petraglia 2011).

As the company was completely unknown, Brunello initially focused not only on the innovative characteristics of the product but also on the quality/price ratio and the punctuality of deliveries. These elements, together with the entrepreneur's brilliance at emphasising the garments' Umbrian origin, enabled a rapid growth in turnover in northern Italy and in the Austrian and German markets.

8.2 The development of products and international markets

In the second half of the 1980s, there was an expansion in the supply of products for customers and entry into some of the most important foreign markets, thanks to the development of a multi-brand wholesale distribution channel (top department stores and speciality stores in the United States, Europe and Asia: Neiman Marcus, Saks Fifth Avenue, Bergdorf Goodman, Harrods, Isetan/Mitsukoshi and Shinsegae).

In the mid-1980s, Cucinelli bought a share in Rivamonti, a company specialising in the creation and production of wool knitwear, and subsequently became a partner in Gunex: the Brunello Cucinelli cashmere knitwear was joined by wool knitwear under the Rivamonti brand and trousers under the Gunex label. In the mid-1990s, Brunello Cucinelli's first menswear collection was launched and the first Brunello Cucinelli shop opened in Porto Cervo. At the beginning

Figure 8.2 **The 'total look' for men and women by Brunello Cucinelli.**

Source: Courtesy of the Brunello Cucinelli company.

of the second millennium, Brunello began to develop ideas for a 'total look' (Fig. 8.2): although the company's activities remained focused on cashmere knitwear, new products began to be developed (men's shirts, women's blouses, outerwear for men, clothing for women and accessories like handbags and shoes) to complement the knitwear collections. In addition, Brunello's desire to retain control of production and marketing, in order to ensure the utmost quality and exclusivity, led him reject the option of licensing his brand names to third parties. In this period the brand's stylistic identity was refined, allowing the company to be successful at an international level, not only alongside more long-standing cashmere specialists such as Loro Piana, Malo and Ballantyne, but also gaining a particular space and positioning among specialist luxury brands.

In the early 2000s, the development strategy of the firm focused on the opening of flagship stores both as franchises or under direct management in Italy and abroad. Shops bearing the Brunello Cucinelli sign opened on the most prestigious streets in major Italian and foreign cities, and in some very exclusive resorts. Among the directly managed flagship stores are those in Milan, Paris, New York, Shanghai, Miami, Madrid, Capri and St Moritz, and those managed by franchise include shops in Rome, London, Tokyo, Moscow, St Petersburg, Cortina and St Tropez.

To promote international expansion, several foreign subsidiaries directly control both retail and wholesale distribution channels in the United States, Germany, Spain and France. In Japan, China and Russia, commercial joint ventures have been set up with important local distribution partners.

As from the autumn/winter 2011–12 collection, the Rivamonti and Gunex brands were discontinued and the group's entire range, which continues to cover all the categories mentioned previously, is brought to market under the unifying brand of Brunello Cucinelli.

By the end of 2011, the group's total turnover reached €242 million, with an EBITDA of over €40 million. There are 715 direct employees, mostly at the headquarters in Solomeo, but with a growing number of employees in the foreign commercial branches. In addition, the company uses a network of over 300 external *façonisti*, mostly located in Umbria, making a satellite industry of over 3,000 employees.

8.3 The village of Solomeo and the relationship with the territory

After spending its early years in a small industrial warehouse, the company transferred its headquarters to the small and half-derelict 14th-century village of Solomeo, a few kilometres from Perugia (Fig. 8.3), where Brunello's wife Federica was born. The son of a farmer who then became a factory worker, Brunello initially trained as an engineering student. He has a strong aesthetic sense and a great passion for medieval

Figure 8.3 **The village of Solomeo.**

Source: Courtesy of the Brunello Cucinelli company.

Umbrian architecture: he realised that his company base should express the culture of his homeland and be a mutual source of inspiration for him, his employees and his collaborators. For this reason, even though he had few resources, he gradually bought a cluster of ruined buildings and land close to the castle and started restoration works which also involved the parish church. A significant share of the company's profits was then allocated to the village project, a demonstration of the tight integration between the company and its territory. Solomeo has become one of the hallmarks of the company, to the extent that the village's coat of arms bearing an image of the castle is used on the Brunello Cucinelli label and has become the company logo. Today in Solomeo, after impressive and passionate restoration work by professionals and local craftsmen directly supervised by the entrepreneur, we find the true heart of the company. Brunello defines himself more as a 'guardian' than the 'owner' of the castle and main buildings close by which, besides being the company's headquarters, have now become a tourist destination thanks to the attraction of a factory outlet store.

In recent years the village of Solomeo has been enriched with other important achievements, such as the Cucinelli Theatre (Fig. 8.4), the Forum of the Arts (Fig. 8.5) and the Neo-Humanist Academy. The design of the theatre is inspired by ancient Greek gymnasiums where young people were educated in music and the arts and practised gymnastics. The Forum of the Arts is a place to meet others and for creativity and culture, the result of joint work intended to enrich

Figure 8.4 **The Cucinelli Theatre.**

Source: Courtesy of the Brunello Cucinelli company.

Figure 8.5 **The Forum of the Arts.**

Source: Courtesy of the Brunello Cucinelli company.

the community and provide heritage for future generations. 'I am not interested in it becoming a multifunctional room, but rather a place of culture and quality. In this theatre I want things that are good for people, nothing that makes the soul ugly' (Mariani 2012). Inside the Forum of the Arts is an amphitheatre which hosts open-air cultural events and performances. It also includes the the Philosophers Garden, which sits on a series of terraces overlooking the Umbrian valley. The Neo-Humanist Academy and its library, a classical-style structure adjoining the Forum of the Arts, were inaugurated in 2010 and provide a venue for professional, craft and managerial training, business meetings and cultural enrichment courses.

8.4 Humanistic philosophy and the concept of labour

'Beauty will save the world.' This phrase by the Russian philosopher and writer Dostoevsky welcomes visitors to the Brunello Cucinelli website and is also the base on which the company's cultural heritage is built.

Brunello Cucinelli's corporate philosophy is expressed by a model which places people at the centre of the production process and allows a sense of participation in the company's success. This model is shared at all levels of the company and in external relations with *façonisti*, suppliers, agents and customers, and translates into a strong level of loyalty and involvement. Both inside and outside the company, human values are always paramount. Brunello's philosophy is rooted in the teachings of his father who, as a farmer and factory worker, always taught him to have highest regard for human dignity. These values have then been cultivated with readings of the ancient philosophers and teachers: Socrates, Aristotle, Seneca, Alexander the Great, Marcus Aurelius, St Benedict, St Francis, St Augustine, Dante and Palladio. In this humanistic Solomeo enterprise, people are seen as the supreme good of the company and profit is not considered a goal in itself, but as a means to make the company stronger and to allow the people who work there to live fully according to nature and to 'follow virtue and knowledge'. The pursuit of beauty is revealed in all the company's activities: the buildings which house the head-quarters, the shops and corporate showrooms, product design, visual merchandising and advertising campaigns must all convey the soul of Solomeo and its surrounding territory, as well as attending to the inner spirit of those who participate in the life of the company. When attending the sector's main trade fairs such as Pitti Uomo in Florence and CPD in Düsseldorf, every important buyer in the world can recognise Brunello's team of collaborators from afar by their clothes, courtesy, 'style' and how they move around. Pride for the company's Umbrian origins is also reinforced by the traditional local food, sweets and wines which are always to hand at national and international fairs, business events and press conferences.

The company philosophy of the Brunello Cucinelli group is also expressed through great attention to the beauty of the workplace. The design office is located inside the castle tower, with medieval frescoes on the walls and wonderful views overlooking the Umbrian countryside: the colour palette used in Cucinelli's collections—mostly shades of grey, brown and white, the colours of the earth and nature, the shades of marble and stone—is obviously the result of inspiration from the *genius loci*. In addition, some extremely skilful craft activities such as quality control and link stitching are located within beautiful wings of the castle dressed with beams, stones and decorative bricks, which offer an appropriate setting for the skilled manual workers. In the environs of the castle, the company has a restaurant/canteen serving traditional Umbrian dishes, respecting the culinary and social traditions of the meal which are so important in local culture. The numerous customers who come at the weekend to shop at the company's outlet store and to visit Solomeo are welcomed in the restaurant with great simplicity and friendliness.

The presence of the Theatre, the Forum of the Arts and the Neo-Humanist Academy brings employees closer to art, crafts and culture. Brunello personally encourages employees not to stay at the office after a certain hour so they can dedicate time to sport, to cultural and recreational activities, and to their families.

This climate stimulates exchange, creativity, speed and liveliness within work groups and, ultimately, the dynamism of the company, which can benefit from the transmission of specific intellectual and manual knowledge. For some craft activities, like that of link stitching, the company organises special training courses in which the most skilled workers teach young people their trade secrets, ensuring the continuity not only of technical and manual know-how but also of pride and passion for the job. Company employees, mostly under the age of 30, not only take advantage of expert training, but can also count on a wage which is relatively higher than that of other Umbrian firms. For Brunello Cucinelli, the value of manual crafts and professions assumes a crucial position for the quality of products and for the intrinsic identity of the company. This is why Brunello believes that an economic value should be accorded to artisanal work by paying more than his competitors: manual labour is not perceived as a degrading activity, but rather as a dignified and profitable profession.

> What remains if there are no more artisans working with the passion, dignity, respect, tolerance, curiosity that is the mother of creativity? For the future of my company, I'm more worried about who will know how to continue producing these top-quality products with their hands and minds, than I am about who will buy them.[3]

In addition to the village of Solomeo, another share of the company's profits is also intended to be used, with the consent of employees, for structures and cultural and social works in the surrounding Umbrian territory (Perugia theatre, the Etruscan Arch, the Castel Rigone sports ground, etc.) to reaffirm the company's commitment

3   Brunello Cucinelli, interview with the author.

to humanist values and to create wider approval for the company among the general public and political and cultural institutions. For this reason, Brunello Cucinelli regularly receives prizes and awards not only for his entrepreneurial achievements, but also especially for the cultural initiatives which he promotes and for his particular organisational model centred on human values. In 1998, he was awarded the title of 'Academic' by the Institute of Fine Arts in Perugia for his dual vocation of entrepreneur and philosopher, and for always having devoted shares of his profits to cultural activities. In 2003, the 'Biella Cultura' Academy awarded him the recognition of 'Homo Faber—Homo Poeticus', given each year to an Italian entrepreneur demonstrating a strong connection with the cultural world. In 2009 and 2010 he received the 'Imprenditore Olivettiano' award and the 'Valorisation of the Territory' award from Confindustria (the main association representing manufacturing and service companies in Italy) for having created and developed an internationally successful Italian industrial group based on fundamental values such as respect for people, a constant quest for products of beauty, love for the environment and for the Umbrian territory, promotion of art and commitment to the rebirth of Solomeo. In 2010, he received the title of 'Order of Merit for Labour' from the Italian president, Giorgio Napolitano, and an honorary degree in Philosophy and Ethics of Human Relations from the University of Perugia.

8.5 The organisational model and employee relations

The Cucinelli Group operates an organisational model in which product strategies and communication activities are closely linked, in order to be consistent with Brunello Cucinelli's image and style.

The distinguishing feature of the business's management is the great importance to time spent collectively sharing issues which concern the life of the company, which translates into management carried out through the establishment of specific boards and committees which have the task of identifying and setting out the company's guidelines. A 'Council of Fifty' meets on an annual basis to communicate in detail the strategies and objectives planned within the group's sphere of operations, and the Development Council, comprising the top managers, which meets every month to agree the management plans for activity. These are followed by several committees of a more operational character which meet more frequently: the Management Committee, which processes the management plans; the Human Resources Committee, which addresses issues relating to policy and development, training and valorisation of human resources; and the Architectural Design Committee, comprising three members of the company and two external architects, which discusses Brunello Cucinelli design and taste even with regards to product display (shops, showrooms and subsidiary offices).

The corporate project is shared with all employees, who are involved in the scope and strategies of the business through participation in quarterly meetings in which the most important results and decisions are discussed. In recent years, in line with the company's growth, younger people have joined with a higher cultural and educational level than former members, and they have been able to integrate into the company's culture by means of these intense and frequent mechanisms for information, sharing and involvement. In addition, especially for younger employees, great importance is given to intense, daily training, which facilitates the transfer of intellectual and manual know-how.

The company is not organogramatically structured and nor does it have excessive levels of hierarchy: of course, there are precise points of reference (members of the Development Council) for the various corporate processes, but teamwork and individual responsibility for results are favoured. For this reason, employees have free access to the workplace, do not have to clock in and can use the outside spaces, such as the park and the orchard, for recreation.

Brunello Cucinelli's philosophy and humanistic principles, resulting from over 30 years in business, are synthesised in a code of ethics in which the values and responsibilities which have always distinguished the entrepreneurial culture of the company are set clearly set out. The same process of 'sharing the profits' is consistent with the philosophy and guiding principles of the company:

> We always divide the end-of-year profits into five equal parts: one fifth to the company, for renewal and consolidation, one fifth to the shareholders and one fifth to all the employees. The remaining two fifths are assigned to the village of Solomeo and to cultural, social or humanitarian activities which are decided together with all the employees.

Code of ethics of Brunello Cucinelli SpA

General principles

The following is a list of the principles and values deemed to be fundamental, to which the various stakeholders are to refer in order to foster the Company's efficient operation, reliability and reputation.

Legality. In conducting its business, the Company acts in a manner compliant with all laws and regulations in force in the territories in which it operates, as well as with the Code of Ethics and Company procedures, which it applies with integrity and equity.

Confidentiality. The Company guarantees the confidentiality of the personal information and data it processes and the protection of information obtained in regards to professional services rendered.

Transparency. The Company undertakes to provide all stakeholders with a clear and transparent account of its situation and performance, without favouring any group of interests or individual.

Fair competition. The Company operates on the Italian and international market in the sale of cashmere knitwear, articles of apparel in leather and other materials, and accessories, and engages in fair competition

→

in the marketplace, complying with Italian and European principles and laws protecting competition.

Personal dignity. The Company undertakes to promote respect for the physical and cultural integrity of individuals and respect for interpersonal relations. It guarantees working conditions that are respectful of Individual's dignity and safe working environments and safeguards and promotes the value of human resources, all with the aim of improving and increasing the wealth of skills possessed by each employee.

Integrity and propriety. Dealings with the Company's stakeholders are guided by the principles of propriety, cooperation, loyalty and mutual respect. External relations and employee relations are shaped by the utmost sense of loyalty, which consists in acting with a sense of responsibility.

Quality. The Company undertakes to be attentive to the market's changing needs and to constantly improve the quality of its products.

Environmental protection. The Company contributes constructively to environmental sustainability in all of its activities. The commitment to safeguard the environment is put into practice by planning activities that seek a balance between economic initiatives and essential environmental needs in accordance with applicable Italian and international directives.

Responsibility to society. In its operations, the Company takes account of the needs of the community in which it conducts its business and contributes to promoting quality of life as well as economic, social, cultural and civil development.

Source: Excerpt from *Code of Ethics of Brunello Cucinelli, approved by the Board of Directors on June 20th, 2011,* http://investor.brunellocucinelli.com/php/fileDownload.php?id=144.

8.5.1 The relationship with suppliers and *façonisti*

Brunello Cucinelli stocks raw materials exclusively from Italian suppliers, the only exception being denim, of which the best quality comes from Japan. With regards to cashmere, the areas of origin are China and Mongolia and he avails himself of three Italian suppliers. The most important, Cariaggi Lanificio, is a Marche-based supplier with which the company has been collaborating for over 20 years. There are also specific multi-year agreements with suppliers to provide the highest quality yarn, at agreed prices according to quantity, taking into consideration exchange rates and fluctuations in the prices of the raw material. Cariaggi also provides cashmere dyes to the company, based on Cucinelli's technical specifications. Cucinelli is one of the supplier's main customers, so the relationship, endorsed by personal contact between the two owners, transcends the classic supplier–client relationship and can therefore be considered a true partnership in which both parties grow together, developing innovation and quality, and sharing the economic risks associated with the international market for raw materials and with currency trends.

For the production of clothing and accessories, Brunello Cucinelli relies on an extensive network of *façonisti*, providing them with the raw materials purchased from his suppliers. The fundamental and characteristic element of the production and logistics phase is the constant and meticulous quality control exercised throughout the entire production process, both for items of clothing and accessories. The *façonisti*, comprised of over 300 companies with around ten employees each, have been in business for an average of about 40 years and are considered an integral part of the business and a key resource for product and service quality. Many of them are engaged under multi-year framework agreements and the company routinely provides support and advice on necessary investment, the personnel to be trained and on the funding opportunities directly available from Cucinelli financial institutions. These agreements stipulate that the *façonisti* comply with the high standards which epitomise Brunello Cucinelli products, as well as correctly remunerating the staff involved in the work and, in general, strictly adhering to enforced regulations concerning social security, welfare, safety, insurance, tax and waste disposal.

At least once a year, before Christmas, all the *façonisti*, represented by their senior and junior owners, are invited by Brunello to a large theatre for an event entirely in their honour: the company shows them how the company's activities are progressing (especially to reassure them about continuity of work), presents the strategies currently under way, and entertains them with visiting speakers not only on important economic issues but also social and ethical topics, making them feel part of a great community. At the end of the evening, Brunello greets the guests one by one, thanking them for their involvement and personally wishing them and their families a happy holiday season.

8.6 The communication strategy

Since the early days, Brunello Cucinelli has made a great effort to define a communication strategy to support the brand's image in an apposite fashion. The structuring of the communication strategy is consistent with the fundamental values that characterise the company's philosophy, in which the efficiency of the industrial organisation is associated with economic ethics and extols the virtues of art, creativity, harmony and a sense of beauty. The communication strategy of the group focuses on three levels:

- Communication of the values and the corporate philosophy on which the Cucinelli Group is based

- Communication of the product

- Communication of the brand

The communication activities, discreet and unnoticeable, are carried out through the media of the luxury market, i.e. magazines which specialise in the sector together with newspapers, and is characterised by a strong innovative drive. In fact, advertising campaigns are mainly evocative and not merely commercial; associated with cultural

Figure 8.6 **Brunello Cucinelli advertisement for autumn/ winter 2012.**

Source: Courtesy of the Brunello Cucinelli company.

and philosophical topics, they are especially designed to communicate and transfer the brand's value by presenting the image of a particular lifestyle (Fig. 8.6).

An integral part of the group's communication strategy is the support provided for wholesale customers (mono- and multi-brand) and to the directly operated stores by making in-store material available, including the collections' catalogue. The catalogue is very carefully presented with regards to the type of paper and the artistic photographs reproduced inside, which transmit creativity, craftsmanship, lifestyle and quality of life.

The communication strategy adopted by the group has generated a good return over the years, as demonstrated by the high number of editorial pieces appearing in the media for each page of paid advertising. The national and international press pays great attention to the brand which, in 2011, managed to get more than 3,000 editorial pieces published. In that year, as shown by analysis provided by Digital Media Research, the return of editorials on advertising investment was 6.2:1 (i.e. for each page of paid advertising, 6.2 editorial pieces were published), much higher than the industry average.

8.7 The stock market listing

April 2012 saw a major breakthrough for the company following Brunello Cucinelli's decision to list the group on the stock market by selling around 30% of shares in the business. Cucinelli's choice is particularly critical as it is well known that, in general, financial markets are more geared towards evaluating economic and financial performance rather than the philosophy and ethics of listed companies. The entrepreneur describes the motivation behind his decision:

> I did it to gain more visibility, to attract top managers to Solomeo more easily. To stand comparison with my investors, who have a slightly different way of thinking than me, I wanted them to gather in Solomeo a few months before the listing, in order to let them touch and see for themselves the reality that we have built over these years. Furthermore, I made this choice to have a more capitalised company and new financial resources to grow. Lastly, my age. I believe that the listing can make this company live longer, for a few decades at least. Then, if my daughters will prove capable, it will be their turn to lead it on a new course (Iozzia 2012).

The company cited its key factors for success during the listing as follows.[4]

- *A strong brand identity.* Positioned at the top of the luxury pyramid, the Brunello Cucinelli brand is internationally recognised as one of the prime examples of 'absolute luxury'. It combines superb Italian manufacturing with the ability to innovate

4   Prospectus for admission to the stock market, April 2012.

and set trends, while preserving the identity of taste and style focused on the 'informal luxury total look'.

- *Product excellence and centrality.* The attention and care that have gone into manufacturing the product are evident in the use of superb raw materials, a sartorial approach, artisan craftsmanship carried out exclusively in Italy, and a meticulous and constant quality control of the entire production process.

- *The widespread appeal and modernity of the Brunello Cucinelli style.* Thanks to its understated yet contemporary style, a great ability to 'listen' to the market, and the exclusiveness and creativity that distinguish the products, the company is able to produce a line that satisfies the tastes of a broad customer base in terms of age and lifestyle.

- *A humanistic philosophy and company.* An ethical and humanistic entrepreneurial model places people at the centre of the production process. It encourages the creativity of each worker and simultaneously develops within them a sense of profound participation in the group's success and goals. This commitment is shared at all levels of the company and in external relations with *façonisti* and with clients around the globe, creating a strong level of loyalty and trust towards the company.

- *Communication strategy.* A precise, targeted communication strategy aimed at conveying and promoting the intrinsic qualities of the product, the artisan approach and the creativity, together with the importance of tradition and the company philosophy, has created an alluring aura of authenticity and uniqueness around the brand which expresses the 'art of living' and 'natural luxury'. All this has generated interest in the national and international press, as shown by the returns, which are above average for the sector, in terms of editorial pieces and mentions of the brand.

- *Organisational model.* Outstanding know-how developed within the company, combined with a network of qualified external artisan workshops (mainly in Umbria), is at the basis of a flexible and integrated organisation which is supported daily by the sales and visual merchandising teams. The company is known for the quality and timeliness of production, the constant control of its value chain, its punctual deliveries, and customer satisfaction.

- *A distribution policy based on selectivity and exclusivity.* The continuous development of a particularly selective distribution network achieved by opening mono-brand stores in the luxury shopping districts of world capitals and in the most famous and exclusive resort locations, and the targeted selection of space in major department stores and international multi-brand stores, have made it possible over time to strengthen the brand's exclusive positioning and brand recognition at a global level.

- *A 'total look' product range.* Besides being a leader in the design and production of cashmere knitware, the group has developed new product categories, preserving the integrity and uniqueness of the Brunello Cucinelli brand and style and focusing on the complementary aspect of products in Brunello Cucinelli collections.

- *A multichannel distribution network.* The group can count on several different distribution channels that guarantee its presence on the market. Its growth is ensured by a balanced combination of distribution channels, including retail and multi-brand wholesale. On 31 December 2011, the group was present on the market with 20 directly operated stores, 39 franchised shops and over 1,000 multi-brand shops. Furthermore, from 2011, Brunello Cucinelli began selling its products online under the management of the Yoox Group.

- *Diversified geographical exposure.* Brunello Cucinelli has a consolidated presence in Europe, the United States and Japan. In recent years, the group has also expanded its presence in China and other emerging markets.

The Brunello Cucinelli board of directors comprises nine members; among them, in addition to the president and CEO, Brunello Cucinelli, are some former members and managers of long standing in the company, some external managers and entrepreneurs with an extremely high international profile, and also Fr Cassian Folsom, who recently joined as an independent director. This is his profile:

> Fr Cassian Folsom, OSB, was born in Lynn (Massachusetts) in 1955. He became a monk in 1980 at St Meinrad Archabbey (Indiana) and in 1981 concluded his religious studies at Indiana University. He was ordained as a priest in 1984. He earned a PhD in Liturgy from the Pontifical Liturgical Institute at Sant'Anselmo (Rome) in 1989. He taught liturgical theology at St Meinrad School of Theology from 1989 to 1993 and was also choirmaster of St Meinrad Archabbey choir. He became a teacher (*Consociatus*) at the Pontifical Institute of Sacred Liturgy in 1993. He was pro-president of the Pontifical Institute of Sacred Liturgy and vice-rector of the Pontifical Atheneum of St Anselm from 1997 to 2000. He was the editor of *Ecclesia Orans* from 1997 to 1998. From 1998 to the present he has been the prior of the Monastery of St Benedict, Norcia, Italy. From December 2000 to the present he has been the rector of St Benedict's Basilica (Norcia). He became a consultant (*consultor*) for the Congregation for Divine Worship and the Discipline of the Sacraments in 2010. He has written many books on the subject of liturgy.[5]

> I just wanted to have someone on the Board of Directors who could give the other directors his own contribution on the philosophical, humanistic and ethical dimension of the company, which is so important for safeguarding and possibly strengthening it. I have known Fr Cassian for several

5   Prospectus for admission to the stock market, April 2012.

years and have had beautiful conversations on philosophy, humanism and religion with him, so I figured that someone like him, with his profound religious values, was the best person to join the Board with such a role.[6]

The share price determined for the listing was fixed at €6.75–7.75, valuing the company at €459–527 million. The launch of the Brunello Cucinelli shares in Piazza Affari, the Italian stock exchange, was very successful: at the beginning of trading the shares rose by 35%, with over a million shares traded in a few minutes. Trading finished early due to demand for shares being 17 times greater than availability, and the final price was fixed at €7.75, at the top of the agreed range. At the end of the first day, the shares had increased by 49.68% to €11.6, about 8 million shares had been traded and a market capitalisation of approximately €780 million achieved. In mid-November 2012, with a share price of around €14, the stock market capitalisation was close to €1 billion. It seems that, as well as end-consumers, employees, suppliers and the local community, even financial markets also appreciate the economic and non-economic performance of the humanistic enterprise from Solomeo.

References and further reading

Iozzia, Giovanni (2012) 'Brunello Cucinelli: la mia filosofia del profitto', *Panorama Economy*, 12 January 2012.

Mariani, Mauro (2012) 'Il Foro delle Arti di Brunello Cucinelli, Industriale Mecenate', *Il Giornale dello Spettacolo* 16, 12 September 2012.

Petraglia, Vincenzo (2011) *Brunello Cucinelli: meglio leggere una poesia che timbrare il cartellino*, http://wisesociety.it/incontri/brunello-cucinelli-meglio-leggere-una-poesia-che-timbrare-il-cartellino/.

6   Brunello Cucinelli, interview with the author.

9
Ethics and fashion: towards a responsible value chain

> This, then, is what the *just is*—the *proportional*; the unjust
> is what violates the proportion. [...] For it is by proportion-
> ate requital that the city holds together. Men seek to return
> either evil for evil [...] or good for good.
>
> Aristotle, *Nicomachean Ethics.*

9.1 The relationship between ethics and the responsible company

The example of Brunello Cucinelli confirms not only that it is possible to bring together apparently contrasting interests within a company, but also the ability to combine various interests—economic,
social and environmental—which can become a source of competitive
advantage. The topic of 'balancing interests' (Fig. 9.1) between different stakeholders in the company has been widely discussed in the
literature (Masini 1979; Coda 2004) and in contemporary debate,
especially in the aftermath of the financial and economic crisis which
has brought into question both the 'ultra-liberal' model of economic

Figure 9.1 **Balancing different interests within the behaviour of the responsible fashion company.**

management and the model of 'maximisation of profit' in company management.

Combining interests means making sure that the different expectations of stakeholders are not exaggerated to the point of one prevailing over the other: if this were acceptable in the short term, even when dealing with contingencies that do not allow all expectations to be satisfied at the same time, in the long term the dissatisfaction of some actors (social and environmental, inside or outside the firm) will inevitably produce negative results, making the actual survival of the company doubtful. The crucial question then becomes, how can we achieve this balance of interests in the long term, subject to the company's need to maintain its economic independence through its ability to produce profit?

Today, ethics and moral values are more topical and form the basis of the behaviour of individuals and the institutions within which they act. However, Adam Smith (1759) suggested that in economics 'compassion must counterbalance selfishness', that 'the moral rules of wisdom, justice, and goodness must be placed before economic interests', and that 'markets do not work without righteous men'. In the past, various authors have proposed a reconceptualisation of business theory along essentially Kantian lines (Evan and Freeman 1988), with a greater attachment to the ethical dimension. More recently, an illustrious Swiss theologian and philosopher (Kung 2010) suggested a theory of 'supremacy of ethics over the economy' (and also over politics), arguing that this is not a 'new concept' but the same classical Aristotelian doctrine according to which the rules of economic rationality must not overwhelm fundamental ethical demands, both secular and religious. In this perspective, as in the philosophy of Brunello Cucinelli's company, man and nature/environment must reassume a central role. As a result, these demands become 'guidelines' for the responsible and virtuous behaviour of the company.

Therefore, entrepreneurs and managers, in the current competitive globalised context, should have a 'threefold competence' (Kung 2010): economic, political and ethical. Political competence deals with the social dimension and the placement of the company in the local, national and international context of institutions and human organisations, while ethical competence deals with the company's own personality, character and system of values.

In particular, company bosses have a responsibility, towards employees and various internal and external stakeholders, to be an 'example' at a moral level and serve as a 'guide' for the behaviour of individuals.

9.2 The specificity of the ethical dimension in the fashion sector

If the ethical dimension, and related social and environmental responsibilities, can create a new model to balance multiple economic and non-economic interests connected to the company, this point of view assumes an even stronger meaning for fashion companies and especially those in Italy. In the fashion industry (clothing, accessories, etc.), the relationship between 'people' (creative designers, technical experts and workers) and 'product quality' is still considerably important, more so for high- and medium/high-end manufactured goods. Thanks to the unique existence of industrial districts for fashion, Italy is the only

Western country to have preserved an industry with a handmade heritage dating back to the Florentine artisan workshops. In no other sector is the process of product innovation so continuous and fast as in fashion: this implies the involvement of many stakeholders in the production chain and distribution network, from raw materials to selling to the end-consumer. It is an involvement which cannot be pursued solely on the basis of economic logic: the passion, motivation, personal gratification and sense of belonging to the company are as important, if not more so, than economic expectations (wages, prices or profits according to who is involved). Moreover, the high level of 'manual labour', such a fundamental element for the recognisability and value of the 'top' products (consider, for example, the hours needed to produce a Hermès or Bottega Veneta bag, a Brioni or Zegna suit, or a Valentino or Armani evening dress), has preserved an importance and ethical dignity in the work that has no equal in more capital-intensive sectors.

9.3 The behaviour of the responsible fashion company

In the previous chapters we stated that a responsible fashion company does not consider the maximising of profit as its sole objective, but balances its own interests with those of numerous stakeholders. In particular, two other objectives guide the company's strategic decisions: to satisfy the social expectations of consumers, suppliers, employees and collaborators, and to reduce environmental impact.

As anticipated, the missing element in this scenario, the glue that can balance the different interests, is ethics: ensuring that economic interests do not clash with those of the stakeholders is a very difficult challenge to overcome if the principles of ethics and morality do not enter into play. In order for man[1] to know what is good for the com-

---

1   'Man' here is intended as those who hold strategic decisional capacity within the company, i.e. the business ownership and top management.

pany, for society and for the environment in which the company is situated, the concept of *homo oeconomicus*—interested in maximising their own wellbeing (advantage)—should be discarded, embracing instead the concept of *homo sociologicus*, who recognises value in the social origin of their 'own' taste and their 'own' functional utility in a broader context than that of the company. Only in this way can we move from a win–lose situation, typical of strategies aimed at the satisfaction of individual interests at the expense of others, to a win–win situation just like a game of co-operation in which the players' interests are not in direct opposition; instead there is a shared interest. The players (companies and stakeholders) pursue a common goal: the maximisation of all stakeholders' welfare.

In game theory, a guarantee is given by binding agreements. More binding rules are surely the most effective way to proceed in order to reach a balancing of interests, but they are not enough in themselves: ethics is the foundation, the root from which decisions must stem. Today, man—the entrepreneur and business manager—is more accountable than ever for actions which are consistent with the final goal: the maximisation of the welfare of all stakeholders, including the environment in which the firm operates. What are these actions? It might be useful to supplement the scheme proposed in Table 2.2. In particular the responsible fashion company (Table 9.1):

- Tries to respect the environment by using raw materials which impact less on the territory and its workers (for example, preferring organic cotton and flax instead of traditional cotton) and optimising the consumption of resources used in production and distribution (energy, water)

- Tries to protect the social territory, workers and consumers while respecting the ILO principles and ensuring a qualitatively satisfactory product

- Tries to increase the consumer's involvement through communication and convey a positive message with authenticity and transparency in order to influence their behaviour, for example

Table 9.1 **Behavioural actions of the responsible fashion company.**

Dimension of context	Stakeholder of reference	Responsible behaviour
Environmental	Environment	• Use raw materials with a lower negative impact on the territory and workers • Optimise the consumption of resources used in production and distribution (energy, water) • Rethink the creative and productive model using cradle-to-cradle logic
Social	Social territory, workers and consumers	• Respect the community of workers, suppliers and employees who collaborate with the company • Comply with the principles set out by the ILO • Respect consumers by ensuring a qualitatively satisfactory product
Media	Media	• Place the consumer at the centre • Use social media and the World Wide Web to inform and involve the consumer • Be authentic and avoid greenwashing and 'ethical washing' campaigns • Start campaigns which influence the consumer (behavioural marketing as in the Patagonia 'Don't Buy This Jacket' or Levi's 'Water<Less Jeans' campaigns
Artistic, cultural and territorial	Art, culture and territory	• Consider culture, landscape and territory as equal stakeholders and start initiatives for their support
Regulatory and institutional	Institutions	• Complying with rules on environmental and social protection is often insufficient: we need a proactive attitude (with respect to voluntary standards and certifications) • Be transparent towards institutions in the narration of one's behaviour
Ethics	All stakeholders	• Reward employees with a fair salary • Respect the human dignity of collaborators and consumers • Respect codes of conduct • Contribute to collective social and civil progress, and to that of the community of reference • Ensure that aesthetics is a bearer of positive values • Trigger a mechanism of responsibility in the value chain

educating them to take care of the product and making them more mindful of the importance of their actions

- Tries to support the culture, landscape and territory in which it is located through concrete and lasting initiatives

- Does not restrict itself to complying with regulations on environmental and social protection, but voluntarily adopts a proactive attitude in respect of more advanced standards, such as those which certify customer guarantees

- Tries in general to adopt an ethical attitude to rewarding employees with a fair salary, to respect the human dignity of collaborators and consumers, to respect codes of conduct, to contribute to collective social and civil progress, and to that of the community of reference, to ensure that aesthetics is the bearer of positive values, and to trigger a mechanism of responsibility in the value chain

9.4 The future of fashion: integrating ethics and aesthetics in the value chain

The ongoing financial and economic crisis in Western countries has accelerated the debate on CSR, to the extent that today it is considered a necessary (but insufficient) condition for competitiveness. For companies in the fashion industry in particular, an important opportunity to regain the confidence of consumers is presenting itself: to restore their value systems and business models by making quality and product innovation the central focus once more.

In the last decade, at a global level, the fashion sector has embraced a variety of different business models and approaches: fast fashion versus the traditional model, volume versus quality, global supply chain versus short supply chain, standardisation versus craftsmanship of the product.

Globalisation has led to the fragmentation of the supply chain, displacing a great part of the manufacturing that was originally carried out locally to developing countries. The mobility of goods and the transport of fibres and yarns from one side of the world to the other have made it increasingly difficult to piece the supply chain together.

Given this variety of business models and approaches, the T&A market is now experiencing a change in key success factors towards quality and responsibility, just like the food sector (as seen with the Slow Food movement).

The responsible company's integration of ethics (value approach) and aesthetics (attention to product quality and innovation) needs to be continually reaffirmed all along the value chain: the principal opportunities include work on product traceability, and on providing the end-consumer with an emotional narrative in response to the increasing desire for guarantees and information about a given product's history.

It still remains to clarify why responsible behaviour can be an advantage for all stakeholders, not just for consumers. If we consider it properly, paying better attention to all company stakeholders also produces better economic performance, especially in the medium to long term, through: the strengthening of reputation (brand equity and brand loyalty), and of the innovative capacity and motivation of suppliers and employees in the value chain; greater employee involvement and loyalty; the development of a positive climate for local communities and society in general; and a positive relationship with the media and public opinion. A responsible attitude therefore stimulates virtuous circle of win–win for all the stakeholders involved.

The best practices presented in this book show how fashion and luxury companies which are responsible and ethical can be 'cool and profitable' at one and the same time, not only by finding an economic balance among all stakeholders, but also by showing themselves to be capable of contributing to economic, social, cultural and moral progress. All this can take place only by deciding to integrate ethics and aesthetics in the value chain.

References and further reading

Arnold, Rebecca (2001) *Fashion, Desire and Anxiety: Image and Morality in the 20th Century* (London: I.B. Tauris).

—— (2009) *Fashion: A Very Short Introduction* (Oxford, UK: Oxford University Press).

Belfanti, Carlo M. (2008) *Civiltà della moda* (Bologna, Italy: il Mulino).

Bendell, Jem, and Anthony Kleanthous (2007) *Deeper Luxury Report* (Goldalming, UK: WWF), www.wwf.org.uk/deeperluxury/_downloads/ DeeperluxuryReport.pdf.

British Fashion Council (2010) *Value of the UK Fashion Industry*, www. britishfashioncouncil.com/content.aspx?CategoryID=1745.

Bulag, Uradyn E. (2010) 'Wearing Ethnic Identity: Power of Dress', in *Berg Encyclopedia of World Dress and Fashion*, vol. 6, *East Asia* (Oxford, UK, and New York, Berg).

Coda, Vittorio (2004) 'Strategia e risorse umane', in Romano Trabucchi (ed.), *Complessità e gestione strategica delle risorse umane* (Milan: Franco Angeli).

Colapinto, John (2011) 'Just Have Less', *The New Yorker*, 3 January 2011.

Commission of the European Communities (2001) *Green Paper. Promoting a European Framework for Corporate Social Responsibility*, www.csr-in-commerce.eu/data/files/resources/717/com_2001_0366_en.pdf.

Dagiliene, Lina, and Rüta Gokiene (2011) 'Valuation of Corporate Social Responsibility Reports', *Economics and Management* 16: 21-7.

De Brito, Marisa, Valentina Carbone and Corinne Meunier Blanquart (2008) 'Toward a Sustainable Fashion Retail Supply Chain in Europe: Organization and Performance', *International Journal of Production Economics* 114: 534-53.

De Monticelli, Roberta (2003) *L'ordine del cuore. Etica e teoria del sentire* (Milan: Garzanti).

Dubois, Bernard, Gilles Laurent and Sandor Czellar (2011) *Consumer Rapport to Luxury: Analyzing Complex and Ambivalent Attitudes* (Paris: HEC), www.hec.fr/var/fre/storage/original/application/5ecca063454eb4e f8227d08506a8673b.pdf.

El Ghoul, Sadok, Omrane Guedhami, Chuck C.Y. Kwok and Dev R. Mishra (2011) 'Does Corporate Social Responsibility Affect the Cost of Capital?', *Journal of Banking & Finance* 35.9: 2388-406.

Evan, William, and R. Edward Freeman (1988) 'A Stakeholder Theory of the Modern Corporation: Kantian Capitalism', in Norman Bowie and Tom Beauchamp (eds.), *Ethical Theory and Business* (Upper Saddle River, NJ: Prentice Hall).

Johnson, Gerry, Kevan Scholes and Richard Whittington (2008) *Exploring Corporate Strategy, Text and Cases*, 8th edn (Harlow, UK: Pearson Education).

Kung, Hans (2010) *Onestà. Perché l'economia ha bisogno di un'etica* (Milan: Rizzoli).

Littrell, Mary A., and Marsha Dickson (2010) *Artisans and Fair Trade: Crafting Development* (Sterling, VA: Kumarian Press).

Lunghi, Carla, and Eugenia Montagni (2007) *La moda della responsabilità* (Milan: Franco Angeli).

Masini, Carlo (1979) *Lavoro e risparmio* (Turin: Utet).

Rees, Kathleen, and Jan Hathcote (2004) 'The US Textile and Apparel Industry in the Age of Globalization', *Global Economy Journal* 4.1, http://dx.doi.org/10.2202/1524-5861.1003.

Ricchetti, Marco, and Maria Luisa Frisa (eds.) (2011) *Il bello e il buono. Le ragioni della moda sostenibile*(Venice, Italy: Marsilio).

Segre Reinach, Simona (2011) *Un mondo di mode. Il vestire globalizzato* (Bari and Rome: Laterza).

Silverstein, Michael J., and Neil Fiske (2003) 'Luxury for the Masses', *Harvard Business Review* 81.4: 48-57.

Smith, Adam (1759) *The Theory of Moral Sentiments* (London).

Turban, Daniel B., and Daniel W. Greening (1997) 'Corporate Social Performance and Organizational Attractiveness to Prospective Employees', *Academy of Management Journal* 40.3: 658-72.

Valli, Bernardo, Benedetta Barzini and Patrizia Calefato (eds.) (2003) *Discipline della moda: l'etica dell'apparenza* (Naples: Liguori).

Veblen, Thorstein (1899) *The Theory of the Leisure Class: An Economic Study in the Evolution of Institutions* (New York: MacMillan).

Ward, David, and Claudia Chiari (2008) *Keeping Luxury Inaccessible* (Munich, Germany: Munich Personal RpPEc Archive).

Willard, Bob (2002) *The Sustainability Advantage: Seven Business Case Benefits of a Triple Bottom Line* (Gabriola Island, Canada: New Society Publishers).

Wilson, Elizabeth (2010) 'Ethics and the Future of Fashion', in Giorgio Riello and Peter McNeil (eds.), *The Fashion History Reader. Global Perspectives* (London and New York, Routledge): 531ff.

Multimedia resources

These multimedia resources have been recommended by Francesca Romana Rinaldi and Salvo Testa. Links to these materials are provided to support teaching, learning and further understanding of some of the concepts and initiatives raised in *The Responsible Fashion Company*.

Greenleaf Publishing does not own any of the following content and is not responsible for the content or delivery of the materials. Other than where specified, the authors do not own the materials.

Articles and videos

Video: Interview with Rachel Hearson, Account Manager, Fairtrade Foundation
www.youtube.com/watch?v=EPZV8ZnCHxk
Original, copyright Francesca Romana Rinaldi

Video: Interview with Yvon Chouinard, Founder of Patagonia
www.youtube.com/watch?v=O3TwULu-Wjw

Video: The Ethical Fashion Show, 2010
http://youtu.be/7Y5KvMOdXv8
Original, copyright Francesca Romana Rinaldi

Video: Copenaghen Fashion Summit
http://youtu.be/NWZVvaSkjXU
Original, copyright Francesca Romana Rinaldi

Article and videos: Francesca Romana Rinaldi on the Copenaghen
Fashion Summit
http://bio-fashion.blogspot.it/2012/05/all-about-youth-fashion-summit-in.
html
Original, copyright Francesca Romana Rinaldi

Video: Andrea Illy's speech at the 'Feeding the World' conference (The
Economist)
www.youtube.com/watch?v=UZKO_6uDzNE

Video: Carmina Campus 'Not charity just work'
www.youtube.com/watch?v=8FW9hS0RsDM

Video: Reggs Design, exploring the concept of 'cradle to cradle'
www.youtube.com/watch?v=4jORau0V62c

Video: Documentary 'Behind the label'
www.youtube.com/watch?v=sN6dGq3m4rY

Video: 'Nike Better World'
www.youtube.com/watch?v=7sggmRi_xx0

Patagonia

Summary and Videos: Patagonia: Environmental and Social Responsibility
www.patagonia.com/eu/enIT/common-threads

Video: Patagonia: Environmental and Social Responsibility
www.patagonia.com/eu/enGB/footprint

Blog posts and videos: The Cleanest Line, Patagonia
www.thecleanestline.com/

Reports

Research Summary and Discussion Paper: The NICE consumer: Toward a framework for sustainable fashion consumption in the EU. Report by the Danish Fashion Institute and BSR
http://youthfashionsummit.files.wordpress.com/2012/03/bsr_nice_consumer_discussion_paper.pdf

Report: CSR in China, India and Brazil 'New Geographies of Corporate Sustainability', Emerging market perspective for Rio+20
https://www.bsr.org/reports/SE124_New_Geographies.pdf

Report: PUMA's Environmental Profit and Loss Account for 2010
http://about.puma.com/wp-content/themes/aboutPUMA_theme/financial-report/pdf/EPL080212final.pdf

About the authors

Francesca Romana Rinaldi is Professor of business strategy in creative industries and fashion management at Bocconi University in Milan. She is faculty member of the Luxury & Fashion Knowledge Center at SDA Bocconi School of Management and the Master in Fashion, Experience & Design Management. Since 2013 she has been Director of the Master in Brand & Retail Experience Management at Milan Fashion Institute (intra-university consortium between Bocconi University, the Catholic University of Milan, and the Polytechnic University of Milan).

She is an international consultant for companies in the fashion and luxury sector, mainly on topics regarding digital strategies, brand management, and business sustainability.

She started the Bio-Fashion blog (http://bio-fashion.blogspot.com) in 2010 with the intention to raise awareness and give information on themes pertaining to fashion and sustainable lifestyles with accounts by firms, opinion leaders, and associations.

A freelance journalist, she contributes to specialist magazines both in Italy and abroad.

Salvo Testa is Professor of business strategies at Bocconi University and SDA Bocconi School of Management, where he created and led the Fashion & Design Platform. Since 2001 he is director of the Major in Fashion & Design conceived by him at the Bocconi University and is professor of Fashion at the same university. For several years he has been Scientific and Executive Counsellor for the Milan Fashion Institute and Director of the Master in Brand & Retail Experience Management. A regular speaker at conferences, panel discussions, and debates on topics related to economy and management of companies in the sectors of fashion, luxury, lifestyle, he is also a management consultant and independent member of board of directors for companies in the sector.

He is author of several publications on the issues of strategy, marketing, product, distribution, communication, and organisation.